C000068209

THE REVEREND LINDA DODDS

Blind
Courage

The story of my father, David Ronald Johnston
1924-1976

THE REVEREND LINDA DODDS

Blind Courage

The story of my father, David Ronald Johnston
1924-1976

MEREO
Cirencester

Mereo Books

1A The Wool Market Dyer Street Cirencester Gloucestershire GL7 2PR
An imprint of Memoirs Publishing www.mereobooks.com

Blind Courage: 978-1-86151-759-3

First published in Great Britain in 2016
by Mereo Books, an imprint of Memoirs Publishing

Copyright ©2017

The Reverend Linda Dodds has asserted her right under the Copyright Designs and
Patents Act 1988 to be identified as the author of this work.

A CIP catalogue record for this book is available from the British Library.

This book is sold subject to the condition that it shall not by way of trade or
otherwise be lent, resold, hired out or otherwise circulated without the publisher's
prior consent in any form of binding or cover, other than that in which it is
published and without a similar condition, including this condition being imposed
on the subsequent purchaser.

The address for Memoirs Publishing Group Limited can be found at
www.memoirspublishing.com

The Memoirs Publishing Group Ltd Reg. No. 7834348

Cover design - Ray Lipscombe

The Memoirs Publishing Group supports both The Forest Stewardship Council®
(FSC®) and the PEFC® leading international forest-certification organisations. Our
books carrying both the FSC label and the PEFC® and are printed on FSC®-certified
paper. FSC® is the only forest-certification scheme supported by the leading
environmental organisations including Greenpeace. Our paper procurement policy
can be found at www.memoirspublishing.com/environment

Typeset in 12/18pt Century Schoolbook
by Wiltshire Associates Publisher Services Ltd. Printed and bound in Great Britain
by Marston Book Services Ltd, Oxfordshire

This book is dedicated to the memory of my wise friend Eileen Welsh (1937 – 2016) who planted a seed.

"Just because a man lacks the use of his eyes doesn't mean he lacks vision"

Stevie Wonder

Contents

Introduction

Dreams

When night has come, and prayers are said,
When peaceful sleep around is spread,
In my dreams, I see again, yes clearly,
The faces of those I have loved so dearly,
God's sunshine, lovely flowers, the birds and the sea,
All come back plainly in dreamland to me.
And I thank my redeemer for being so kind,
For those dreams that give sight to us who are blind.

I found the above poem shortly after the death of my father in 1976, typed on a small piece of thin paper. It was very fragile, and had been folded carefully and placed amongst his personal papers. On first reading it, I admit that it reduced me to tears as I felt the powerful emotion and the deep longing of its simple words. It still holds much emotion for me, but I know the words do not reflect the thoughts of a person who is resentful of their lot in life. The words are not those of someone for whom we need to feel pity or who, indeed, felt any pity for himself. The poem is a simple and truthful statement of the reality of being blind.

The piece of paper remained carefully folded and placed amongst my own treasured possessions for the next forty years. Until, that is, a chance conversation with a dear and good friend Eileen Welsh in which we were reflecting on our childhood days, an exercise more common to us all as we get older, it seems. Eileen, with her usual wisdom and insight, recognised something of interest in the story of my father's life and achievements and of my own experience and perceptions of his blindness. So much so that she persuaded me to give a short talk to the Women's Bright Hour, a small group of now mostly elderly ladies who meet each week at Woodhouse Close Church in Bishop Auckland, and where I was at that time Associate Minister.

During the following few weeks as I thought about what I might say I came across the piece of paper again, unfolded for so many years, carefully placed amongst my own treasured possessions. On reading it I decided that a fitting title for my little talk would be "Being Dad's Eyes".

The talk, much to my surprise, was well received by the ladies. Some of them remembered my father as a prominent figure in the town, well known and recognised, wearing his suit, overcoat and trilby hat, carrying his briefcase and with his guide dog at his side. Their interest and subsequent questions lit the small spark of an idea in my mind and has taken me on the journey of rediscovering my father's story.

We each of us have a story to tell, a story which has formed and shaped us into the person we have become. To each of us our story is our own and represents our own normality. So it was with me. It was only through the interest of my friend that I became aware that maybe my childhood and early life, although normal to me, were perhaps in some significant ways a little different to the experience of others. My story is shaped by my father's remarkable and inspirational life. His story is one of his determination to overcome his own perceived disability and also to challenge the perceptions held by society in respect of the abilities, needs and value of those with sight loss. His is a story of fierce independence fuelled by a deep social conscience which drove him to work tirelessly for the benefit of others, whether in his local community or in the wider world. It is a story as much about sight as the lack of it, about vision and possibilities rather than limitations and restrictions, about ability rather than disability. It is a story fuelled by a determination to prove wrong the attitudes towards disability which were current at that time and to demonstrate that a person's worth and contribution to society are not determined by whether or not they are able to see.

Discovering this story has been a journey which has taken me to times, places and memories which have long lain deep in the recesses of my mind. To venturing into the attic and retrieving boxes of photographs, the faces from the past staring out from the grainy, black and white images. To stories which have leapt from yellowing newspaper cuttings carefully and lovingly pasted into albums. To visits to places, some now long changed from when I first knew them and others which have played significant roles in the story I thought I knew so well and which I was discovering still held surprises. To people who have shared their own memories and brought another dimension to the man who played such a significant part in my life.

There is of course one other person to whom I owe a tremendous amount and whose part in this story has only been truly revealed in its telling, and that is my mother Doreen Lawson, formerly Johnston née Walton.

They say that behind every good man there is a good woman. That is certainly true in my father's case, except that she was not behind him but there beside him, in every sense, literally as she took on the role of being his eyes and metaphorically as she supported and encouraged him and in so many ways enabled him to achieve the remarkable things he did.

This book therefore has been written in memory of both my parents and as a tribute to them. I owe so much of who I am to my father: my social conscience, my sense of the importance of community, my obsession with preparation and organisation, my people-watching skills, my hatred of being late, my offbeat sense of humour and maybe some of my peculiar little habits. And my mother, who was always there in the background and was, as I have discovered, and I hope shines out of these pages as the catalyst who made things possible.

I began with my little talk "Being Dad's Eyes", inspired as it was by the poem I have treasured for so many years. Since that tentative beginning I have gone beyond my own experience to discover the story of a man whose life touched so many others; a man who has time and again been spoken of as inspirational and remarkable. In the light of that the title, "Blind Courage", comes, with permission, from a piece written for the *Northern Echo* by local journalist Mike Amos on his hearing of my father's death.

CHAPTER 1

A routine procedure

My father, David Ronald Johnston, was born at 6 Church Walk, Hartlepool, on the 2nd of May 1924, the eldest child of James Stanley Gladstone Johnston (Stan) and Cordelia (née McKay), although Stan had two other sons, Stanley and Sydney, from a previous marriage.

Stan, who was born in Hartlepool in 1891, worked in the shipyards as a Ship's Plater, as did his father David and grandfather James before him. James Johnston was born in 1844 in Kingshorn, Fife, Scotland. On the 1881 Census he is recorded as living in Jarrow and working as a Boiler Smith in the shipyards. By the 1911 Census he is in Hartlepool still working at the age of sixty-seven and lists his occupation as Marine Boilermaker (Plater).

Cordelia McKay was also born in Hartlepool, in 1899, to Daniel and Cordelia McKay (née Leach). Daniel appears on the 1891 Census aged 27 living in Moreland Street West Hartlepool and also recorded his occupation as Ship's Plater.

The history of Hartlepool is bound up with the sea. Ships have been built there since 1836, when the Hartlepool General Shipping Company built the *Castle Eden*. The last ship, the *Blanchland*, was built in 1961 by William Gray and Company Limited. For over one hundred and twenty years the town has produced ships, from wooden sailing vessels to iron steamships and steel tankers.

The job of a Plater was skilled and heavy work. The outer skin of a ship is made up of metal plates and these often need to have complex curves. The plates have to be bent in three dimensions and the Plater's job was to get the shape right. In modern day ship-building computers have replaced much of the Plater's skill.

The once thriving industry of shipbuilding had supported both the Johnston and Mc Kay families for several generations. By the 1920s, however, there was a severe slump, with job losses and unemployment. By 1924, the year my father was born, William Gray Limited were the only shipbuilders left in Hartlepool, having two berths at Jackson Docks. The economic slump meant that work in the shipyards was very irregular and Stan Johnston, along with his fellow workers, would stand each morning at the shipyard gates hoping to be chosen to work that day. Stan therefore had to find other means by which to supplement his income and support his family when work in the shipyard was slack.

At the time my father was born, he and Cordelia were running a small general dealers shop whilst Stan operated a small fleet of taxis, the only ones in Old Hartlepool at that time, and family lore holds that he drove the first fire engine in the town. If fate had taken a different course, then it is likely that my father would have followed his forebears into the shipyards.

My father was born with full, normal sight and was a healthy baby and toddler. At the age of five he started at Prissick Street School, which is no longer standing. It stood just a couple of streets away from where the family now lived in Friar Terrace.

At the beginning of the 20th century dental health was poor, especially amongst children, so at a conference in 1903 the War Office and the Admiralty argued for dental inspections and oral hygiene instruction in schools. In 1907 the Education (Miscellaneous Provisions) Act instructed local councils to carry out dental inspections at elementary schools.

Whilst undergoing one of these inspections at the school clinic it was discovered that my father needed to have what was presumably a milk-tooth removed. Thinking it to be a routine procedure, his mother agreed to this. Unfortunately it is obvious that there were complications following the extraction of the tooth. My father's mouth and eyes bled excessively and this proved very difficult to stop. In fact the bleeding lasted for five full days, after which it was discovered that the optic nerve had been damaged.

Stan sold his taxi cars one by one in order to find the money needed to allow my Grandmother Cordelia and her friend to take my father to every doctor they could - even travelling to London to see a specialist there. However, the damage to my father's eyes was found to be irreversible; he was totally blind, not even able to distinguish between light and dark. Having had sight for a few of his early years meant that in adulthood he had faint recollections of how some things looked. For example he could remember the shapes of trees. He also had some memory of colours; the blue of the sky and the sea, the green of grass. He carried faint images in his memory of his father and mother as they had been and of his home as it had been when he was five years old, but for the rest of his life he lived in a world of total darkness.

Despite this devastating change in his life, my father seems to have enjoyed a happy childhood. His friend Charles Unthank Lawson, who was a couple of years older than him, lived close by and that friendship deepened, with Charles taking it upon himself from a very early age to be my father's constant companion. He made a point of always being the one who was there for him. They built a relationship which was lifelong and which disregarded any disability my father may have been thought to have. As children they were as adventurous and mischievous as any other boys, never allowing the fact that my father could not see to be any barrier to their childhood games, nor indeed to anything they did together in life. As adults they called each other "Joe" and whenever life or work separated them they kept in constant contact via letters and tape recordings.

It is difficult to appreciate the effect my father's loss of sight must have had on his parents. It most certainly will have changed their lives dramatically. Whether Cordelia ever felt any responsibility for what had happened is unknown. She had taken the advice of the professionals and trusted those she considered to be experts with the safety of her only child. This is something all mothers must face at some time or other, and it is always a time of anxiety and guilt. I feel that it is inevitable that my poor grandmother must have relived many times that moment when the decision to remove my father's "baby" tooth was made and quietly and secretly tortured herself, as all mothers do, over what she maybe could have done differently.

Attitudes to disability in the early 20th century were very different from today. At that time there was a general consensus amongst both the authorities and the general population that every "defective" man, woman and child, a term commonly used, was a burden to the nation to feed and clothe and could produce little or nothing in return. When almost two million newly-disabled ex-servicemen came home from the battlefields of the First World War, however, attitudes slowly began to change.

In the years between 1900 and 1945, up to half a million children had a physical disability or sensory impairment. This was in the main due to poverty or disease, and most working-class parents could not afford specialist equipment or treatment. However, everyone had a right to education, and although some specialist schools could be harsh there were new approaches to the education of blind children. However, although many disabled children were trained for low-skilled work most people thought that they would never find a job (my source is the Historic England website).

My father, however, was fortunate in many ways. Although not well off, his parents were in a position to meet the extra costs and difficulties which having a blind child presented. In addition they appear to have had a very positive attitude to his disability and encouraged my father to have the same outlook, to concentrate on what he was able to do rather than be limited by those things he could not.

In 1889 The Edgerton Commission published a report that recommended blind children should receive compulsory education between the ages of five and sixteen, and the Elementary Education Act of 1893 placed the education of blind and deaf children under the responsibility of Local Authorities. The right to an education was a great step forward for the blind, but there was often an emphasis on low skilled training rather than full education. It was broadly thought at that time that children with disabilities were better off away from their families and so many attended residential schools.

So my father left Prissick Street School and his family home to attend the Royal Victoria School for the Blind in Newcastle. The school had been established from a fund marking the coronation of Queen Victoria in 1837 and at one time was known as the Royal Victoria Asylum. In the 1890s the name was changed to the Royal Victoria School, and in 1895 it moved to a house in Benwell Dene donated by Dr Hodgkin, a notable historian and banker. The school, which provided elementary education, technical training and employment, was residential and took visually-impaired pupils from all over the North of England. It closed in 1985, when moves were made to integrate children with special needs within mainstream education and the house was converted into a hotel.

A glance through the log books reveals that my father appears to have adapted well both to his loss of sight and life at the school. In 1934, aged nine, he is recorded as winning second prize out of eighty entrants in the annual Braille Reading Competition for pupils under the age of twelve held at the National Library for the Blind in Manchester and as winning again the following year. During 1935 he achieved Grades 1 and 2 in the pianoforte examinations and Grade 3 the following year. On May 19th 1936 he was awarded the prize for the April Competition of the Junior Book Club and the following day he was a member of the team which won second prize and Silver Medal in the North of England Musical tournament team reading competition for Elementary Schools.

With my father's future more secure, Stan and Cordelia's life settled back into some sort of normality. They went on to have three more children; Delia Mary, known affectionately as

"Nip" within the family, was born in 1931, Clifford seven years later in 1938 and the youngest, Avis, in 1940.

CHAPTER 2

A wartime education

Pupils who showed the necessary potential were tutored at Benwell to sit the examination for a scholarship from the Gardner Trust for the Blind, which was created in 1879 after Mr Henry Gardner left £300,000 for the benefit of blind persons residing in England and Wales. My father was successful in obtaining a scholarship which was to the value of £40 per annum, a sum which was renewed annually if the recipient's conduct and progress was satisfactory.

Therefore in 1935, at the age of eleven years old, my father left Benwell and the North East to attend the Royal Normal College in London; the word "normal" apparently referring to the teacher training which was on offer there. The college, which was non-denominational, was in Westow Street in Upper Norwood. It was founded in 1872 as an institution exclusively for the blind by the Victorian Philanthropist Dr Thomas Rhodes Armitage and the American Frances Joseph Campbell, taking students from all parts of the British Isles and what were then the colonies. Its purpose was to train blind people to earn their own living and to turn them into independent, self-reliant citizens. Graduates of the college found employment as organists, teachers of music, piano tuners, clergymen, school teachers, governesses and shorthand typists. The introduction to its annual report stated: "without the College training many of them would still be helpless and hopeless and a permanent charge on the rates". The college was founded by voluntary effort and continued to rely on private bequests, and it appears that the need to secure funding in order to continue its work was a constant issue.

Rules on visiting were very strict. Parents and friends were only allowed to visit on alternate Saturdays. If they wished to visit at any other time, then they were required to write to the Principal for an appointment. Only two visitors were allowed at any given time and parents were earnestly requested not to bring young children with them. The rule of no visiting on a Sunday was strictly enforced. Such restrictions must surely have meant that my father received few visits from his family, but when they were able to make the journey it was a great occasion for them all.

In 1939, in accordance with previously made plans to evacuate the college in the event of war, pupils did not return to school in September following the summer break. This was in accordance with previously made plans to evacuate the college in the event of war and the Board of Governors took immediate steps to find suitable wartime accommodation. After much difficulty and many disappointments, they were successful in finding suitable premises in Rolvenden, Kent, in a mansion known as Great Maythem. The house readily lent itself to the school's purposes with the addition of some timber buildings in the grounds which provided music practice rooms, dormitories and washrooms for the older male pupils. Despite the considerable difficulties and expense of moving, the college resumed its work in January 1940. The move from London was not without its advantages, not least the opportunity of enjoying the pleasures and benefits of life in the countryside.

Life at Great Maythem, although now overshadowed by war, seems to have been happy, with pupils and staff providing entertainment through concerts, play readings, piano and song recitals and other social activities. The Governors and Principal were confident that the school could safely continue its valuable work at Great Maythem for the duration of the war.

However the peace and safety of Rolvenden did not last long. The fall of France in June 1940 and the subsequent imminent threat of invasion meant that the area in which the college was situated, formerly a peaceful rural district, was now of military importance. The skies above Kent had become the frontline defence in the war with Germany. As a result the college once again urgently had to seek a new home. Staff and Governors were determined that the outstanding work of the college, with nearly seventy years of outstanding achievement to its credit, should not be allowed to come to an end. However, as no suitable premises were found to be available to rent, the Governors made the decision to purchase Rowton Castle, which had buildings that were adaptable for school use together with extensive grounds and gardens. The evacuation of Great Maythem was done with twenty-four hours' notice and the Royal London Society for the Blind took in the thirty pupils and staff who had remained over the summer holidays at Great Maythem by transferring them to Dorton House, their wartime school near Aylesbury.

Rowton Castle is only a few miles from the Welsh border and is surrounded by beautiful countryside. It is on the site of a former fortress which had been destroyed by the Welsh towards the end of the fifteenth century. The building purchased by the college, whilst containing some original features, dated mainly from the eighteenth and nineteenth centuries. Some reordering of the space was needed in order to accommodate the school's requirements and the wooden huts were brought from Great Maythem to provide additional accommodation.

In the Annual Report of 1940/41 the Principal

states that despite all the anxiety and upheaval of the move to Rowton Castle, life in the school had settled down, pupils and staff were once again enjoying the pleasures of the countryside and its social life was even more than usually active and happy. However, for my father and his family a much more personal tragedy was about to strike. On December 3rd 1940, just a few short months after my father's youngest sister Avis was born, Stan suffered a fatal heart attack whilst working in William Gray's shipyard. He was only 49 years old and his sudden and unexpected death meant Cordelia was left on her own to support four children two of whom were still babies. My father was only sixteen years old and was far away at college in Shrewsbury.

This was a difficult time for the family as the country was in the grip of war and under threat of imminent invasion. It must have been a particularly frightening time for my father being away from his home and his family at such a dark time both in his family's history and that of the country.

Hartlepool had been the first town to be bombarded from the sea during the First World War and its docks and shipyards made it a potential target for attack in the present war. My father must have been very concerned for the safety of his very vulnerable family as they were still living close to the harbour and dockyards. At the time of Stan's death Cordelia and the other three children were living at 6 Baltic Street, a large house adjacent to the fire station, and it seems they were allowed to continue to live there. Such proximity to the fire station did however afford them some measure of safety, as a warning of any imminent air raid received by the firefighters would be also be passed on to the family. This meant they were able to take refuge in the air raid shelter in good time, Nip often carrying her baby sister in a basket fitted with a gas mask resembling a deep sea diver's helmet.

Cordelia received a widow's pension of twenty-one shillings a week to support herself and the three children at home. This was not a lot even for the 1940s, so Cordelia, like Stan before her, had to find other ways to supplement her income. Fortunately the house in Baltic Street, as well as being large, had more than one bathroom, a rare thing in those days. This meant that it was relatively easy to create a couple of almost self-contained apartments, which she then rented out to the captains of ships which anchored in the harbour. With the premature death of her husband, Cordelia must have been greatly concerned not only about her own future but also that of her eldest son. Without Stan there to support them both economically and emotionally the future must have looked frightening and uncertain.

However, despite the death of his father, the separation from his family, the threat of imminent invasion by German forces and the upheaval of evacuation, the annual reports show that my father appears to have thrived at college.

In 1938 he is recorded as winning second prize in a reading competition held at the National Library for pupils between thirteen and sixteen years of age. In 1940 he was the recipient of the "Dixson" Annual Essay Prize and passed the Preliminary Examinations of the British Esperanto Association. In 1942 he received a Credit in the examinations for the Royal Society of Arts Typewriting Stage 1 and a First Class in Stage 2. The same year he passed the examinations for shorthand at 80 words a minute and received a Distinction at 100 words a minute, as well as winning the "Dixson" Annual Essay Prize for a second time. In 1943, his final year, he achieved a Distinction from the London Chamber of Commerce in Shorthand at 120 words a minute, obtained a First Class in Typewriting Stage III, Shorthand at 100 and 120 words a minute and the Shorthand Typist's Certificate, for which he was awarded the Royal Society of Arts Silver Medal. He also achieved a Second Class in English Stage III and was awarded the Type Writing Prize for the best all-round work during the year.

All of my father's studies of course included mastering Braille, the system of transcribing print so it can be read by touch. Although this is now mainly used by blind people, the original idea was apparently for soldiers to be able to read at night without putting themselves in danger by using any light. The system of Braille used in this country was adopted in 1902 and is known as Grade 2. The characters of the standard Braille alphabet are called 'cells' and consist of dots placed on a two-column grid with three positions in each column; there are 64 different cells. Braille however is not just one-to-one with print and the same cells are re-used to have different meanings in different contexts. Braille also uses shorthand symbols called contractions. It is a very complex system and takes a long time to learn and master.

Braille shorthand is based on the same six dots upon which Braille longhand is based but is a highly-contracted form of the latter embodying word signs, letter group signs and outlines. The seven keys on a Braille Shorthand Machine represent the six dots and the space key. The shorthand is embossed onto a continuous roll of tape-paper which passes automatically through the machine with the action of the keys. A speed of 100 words a minute is attained by the average shorthand writer.

CHAPTER 3

Breaking the glass ceiling

At the age of nineteen, fully qualified as a shorthand typist, my father left college in a spirit of confidence and optimism, determined to make his own way in the world. Although providing him with the skills he needed for the world of employment and encouraging him to be independent, his life at boarding school and college had to some degree been sheltered and protected. Naively perhaps, he believed that the outside world would look beyond his disability and recognise and embrace his talents and his ambitions. Sadly this does not seem to have been the case, and although he managed to find continuous employment and live independently, for the next twenty years he appears to have encountered what we might now call a "glass ceiling". In a letter written in June 1969 he referred to this period of his life. Although using the considerable skills he had acquired at college, he was unable to break through the barrier, which restricted him to "being someone's assistant, someone's secretary, the one who helped others to gain recognition or the underdog in one way or another." He described himself as being "alone in a cold and uninterested world which denied me the opportunities I needed".

His determination and savage independence never deserted him, however. He resisted any suggestions from his family and friends that he should consider applying for a guide dog, following their introduction into this country in 1931. He refused even to have the aid of a white stick or to allow anyone to link arms with him. Instead he devised a method of walking alongside in such a way that his shoulder was just slightly behind and touching that of his companion. During a period of working in London he committed the area where he was living to memory, finding his way around by remembering the routes he needed to take and identifying all the obstacles. The thought of him being alone in a large city and finding his way around in such a way must have been a great worry for his family, and particularly for his mother. Even now when I think about it I am filled with dread and wonder in equal measure. However when his future brother-in-law Howard travelled to London to visit, he was amazed at how confident my father was and was able to report back to the family how he had escorted him around the city, pointing out the landmarks, naming all the streets and Underground Stations and negotiating the escalators.

There seems to have been a deep-seated drive within my father which drove him to demonstrate to the world that blind people were at no disadvantage in the workplace, in particular when it came to shorthand and typing, and that their skills could be measured at the same level as any sighted person. And so at the age of twenty, shortly after qualifying from college, he issued a challenge to test his ability against that of any sighted typist in the country. The challenge was taken up by a young lady called Marjorie Weeks, who was employed as a secretary by the National Savings Committee in Manchester. Arrangements were made for the test to take place during the Manchester Back at Work Exhibition in November 1944. This was an event which was aimed at demonstrating that disabled people could make a positive contribution in the workplace, particularly those who had been injured in the Second World War. My father clearly thought it was an appropriate occasion on which to demonstrate his own skills and also to champion the cause of blind people within the workforce.

The two contestants were tested on their ability to take down shorthand at both 120 and 140 words a minute, as well as their transcribing and layout skills. Mr Arthur Cheetham, who was a Pitman's Gold Medallist, was given the responsibility of overseeing the procedures. At the end of the test my father's work was found to equal in every respect that of his sighted opponent both in relative speeds and the ability to transcribe.

"The only point in which these skilled blind typists differ from sighted typists" said an official, "is that they cannot rub out a mistake. They get over that by being so accurate that they never make a mistake." (*The Beacon,* December 15th 1944.)

The Beacon magazine was first published in 1917 and is aimed at health and social care professionals who work with blind and partially-sighted people. Now called *The New Beacon*, it supports the RNIB's focus on prevention, independent living and inclusion.

My father eventually returned to his native North East, although surprisingly not to his home town of Hartlepool. I can only assume this was simply because there was no appropriate work available there. Instead he found work as a telephonist at Westool (The Westminster Tool and Electric Company) in St. Helen's Auckland. The use of a switchboard was part of the curriculum at the Royal College and many blind people found employment as telephonists at that time, as most companies and institutions had their own manually-operated switchboards.

Still maintaining his independence, he found lodgings in Albert Hill in Bishop Auckland, adjacent to the railway station. Charles was a frequent visitor to Albert Hill and the two of them enjoyed the social life of the town and in later life would tell stories of the pranks they played on my father's landlady, Mrs. Howe, who by coincidence was the grandmother of my friend and inspiration Eileen Welsh.

However, although he was very efficient at the job, my father did not settle to being a telephonist, so after a time he applied for and secured the position of Personal Secretary to Leo Lewin, head of the West Auckland Clothing Company, which was also in St. Helen's. The firm, which had a showroom in London, manufactured popular medium-priced ladies' clothing, mainly coats. As this new position came with a key worker's house my father brought his mother, brother and sisters from Hartlepool to live in Dalton Avenue on the nearby newly-built housing estate. In doing so he quickly assumed the role of head of the household and a father figure to his siblings. In a reversal of roles, his mother sought his guidance in all family matters and decisions and he became her companion, confidant and advisor. Similarly his brothers and sisters looked up to him as the person they turned to whenever they were in need of advice or support.

On his return to the North East my father began to form friendships and business acquaintances with other blind and partially-sighted people in the area. Although attitudes to disability in general were slowly changing following the Second World War, there was still a general misconception within society about the needs and abilities of blind people. They were still considered by many as being separate from society as a whole and unable to participate fully in the social, cultural and economic activities of their communities.

This was an issue about which my father was passionate, so in May 1950 he founded the North Eastern Area Social and Cultural Organisation for blind persons and their sighted friends.

NASCO, as it was known, was at that time the only organisation of its kind. Membership was open to both blind and fully-sighted persons, provided that the number of sighted members did not exceed the number of those who were blind. My father described NASCO as having two principal aims: firstly to dispel the popular tendency to regard blind people as a community apart, and secondly to provide them with facilities which would not otherwise be available to them.

During the winter the group met together once a month in Durham City for such things as lectures by well-known speakers, concerts, recitals, dances, socials and other similar activities. In the summer the programme included weekend camps, bird-watching and coach tours. The group purchased an old double-decker bus, which they sited near the River Wear in Durham City. The top deck was converted into bedrooms, the cab into a small kitchen and the lower deck into a communal area for relaxing, playing cards and dominoes etc.

Isolation was often a reality for many blind people, so these activities gave them an opportunity to meet with other people, both blind and sighted, in a social setting. As the name suggests, there was a deliberate attempt to provide members with access to cultural activities as well as opportunities just to have fun together.

To this end they formed a cricket team which played in a local league. This gave members the opportunity to participate in a team activity, which helped to build up confidence and self-esteem. The NASCO cricket team was made up of seven fully-sighted members and four blind players. Their opposing teams were always composed of fully-sighted players, and the only concession made to the blind players was the use of a ball with a bell in it. The team seem to have been quite successful; during the 1953 season they won nine matches, drawing one and losing one.

CHAPTER 4

Love and marriage

My mother, Doreen Walton, was born in Leadgate, near Consett, on the 12th of September 1927, the only surviving child of Joseph Harrison (Harrie) and Constance (Connie, née Saxty). Her elder sister Sarah had died at the age of five before my mother was born.

Her father's family had lived for generations in

Weardale, working as auctioneers and lead miners in St. John's Chapel and Stanhope. Her grandfather, Joseph Walton, after serving an apprenticeship as a saddler with his uncle in Wolsingham, moved to Hexham in Northumberland, where her father was born. Her maternal grandfather, Henry James Saxty, was born in Edinburgh and on the 1881 Census is recorded as working as a plumber at the Consett Ironworks.

Harrie Walton was a Master Grocer and worked as a manager for Walter Willson's Ltd, which owned grocery stores throughout the North East and Cumbria. His work meant that he travelled around the North East, often being sent to turn around the fortunes of stores which were failing, so the family moved house many times. By the 1950s however, the family were settled and living in Station Road, West Auckland and my mother was working as a cashier for the London and Newcastle Tea Company. This was one of the UK's earliest chain stores and had a branch in Newgate Street, Bishop Auckland. They had a loyalty scheme, long before Tesco Points were thought of, giving a brass token with each order of tea. Customers saved the tokens until they had enough to claim a prize such as a toy, an item of crockery or a household gadget.

By this time my father had changed jobs again and was now working as a secretary in the Planning Department at Ashmore, Benson, Pease & Co. Ltd, engineers and iron founders in Stockton. The story of how my parents met is an unusual and rather romantic one. Part of my mother's job was to call in the evenings at customers' houses collecting their orders for tea and other groceries. The area she covered was West Auckland and St. Helen's Auckland and one of the houses on her round was 17 Simpson Avenue in St Helen's, which was where my father and his family were now living. My mother would call at the house to collect

Cordelia's order each week and presumably they chatted for a while on the doorstep about the weather, discussing her order and the like. From the inside of the house my father happened to hear one of these conversations and liking the sound of my mother's voice, he contrived to be the one who answered the door the next week when she called. Following several conversations on the doorstep my father invited her out, and their romance blossomed from there.

My father was always proud to say that he fell in love with my mother's voice. He had had a few girlfriends before he met my mother but nothing serious. However, he obviously recognised something special in her, something intangible that was there in her voice. Most of their courting seems to have been within the social activities of NASCO; dances, fancy dress balls, overnight walks, and the cricket team. My mother it seems turned out to be quite a good fielder and took up the position of silly mid-off.

My parents were married in the historic church of St Helen, Auckland, on August 3rd 1953, which was Bank Holiday Monday, as her father could not be persuaded to take a Saturday off from work. The ceremony was conducted by Rev. W. Richardson, Vicar of St. Helen's and a personal friend of the Waltons. Charles was Best Man, my father's brother Cliff a groomsman and sister Avis a bridesmaid. Sixty-eight members of NASCO, sighted and unsighted, attended the wedding, including the members of the Cricket Team.

Harrie and Connie were now living in the part of the vicarage which had once been the servants' quarters and so my mother donned her dress of ivory watermarked silk with a three-yard train, a veil of French silk net and a coronet of orange blossom in one of the bedrooms of the vicarage. Carrying a bouquet of red roses, she fulfilled her dream by sweeping down the broad vicarage staircase on her way to church.

Reports of their wedding appeared in several

newspapers, both local and national. Most inevitably focused on the fact that my father was blind, as well as references to his shorthand and typing achievements and his founding of NASCO. The romantic way in which they had met also provided a good story line. The *Daily Mirror* reported it on August 3rd under the heading "He fell in love with her cheerful voice":

Every Thursday Doreen Walton, 25, called at No. 17 for the grocery order. Usually Mrs. Johnston, the occupier of No. 17 went to the door. But one day her son David, who has been blind for more than twenty years, answered the bell. He liked Doreen's cheery voice so much, he was at the door when she called the next week. And the week after... And many more weeks. He took her to a party for the blind folk and their friends...Then the romance blossomed, though in his home at Simpson Avenue, St. Helen's, Bishop Auckland, Co. Durham he can only "picture" her by tracing the contours of her face with his sensitive hands.

So yesterday Doreen was having the last-minute fitting of her wedding dress for the ceremony in St. Helen's Church today.

"I suppose I will be his eyes for the rest of our lives," said Doreen, blue-eyed brunette, "but I am not marrying a helpless person by any means. All David was worried about was whether I had a fat face, so he traced my features to make sure."

This is the only time I have heard my father referred to as David or my mother call him by his first Christian name; he was always known within the family as Ron. Following the wedding my mother moved in with the family in Simpson Avenue, as Nip and Howard had been married the previous year and were now living in nearby Auckland Park.

My father continued to work tirelessly to encourage the public to look beyond a blind person's disability and to appreciate his or her skills. He also aimed to help other blind people realise that nothing was impossible and that the lack of sight did not prevent any blind person with a reasonable education becoming an efficient shorthand typist.

Following the success of the contest in Manchester and in an attempt to raise local awareness of the abilities of blind people, and in particular blind shorthand typists, he organised an event which was held in the Newgate Methodist Church Hall in Bishop Auckland. On display was an exhibition of shorthand and typewritten work done by blind people. My father himself gave demonstrations of the ability of sightless people with a Braille shorthand machine and a typewriter. On show at the exhibition were examples of work done by students of the College of the Blind, and these included typed programmes, menus, commercial work and pictures of Rowton Castle created by the use of different keys on a typewriter.

I was born on September 21st 1954 and my arrival was apparently of some concern within the family, especially to my maternal grandparents, who were worried, justifiably maybe, that having a child to look after along with caring for my father would be too much extra responsibility and work for my mother. She of course just took it all in her stride, becoming carer, mother, cleaner, decorator, odd job person and gardener all rolled into one.

After much pressure from family and close friends however, my father was finally persuaded to apply for a guide dog and in January 1955 he went to the Guide Dogs for the Blind Training Centre in Leamington Spa, Warwickshire, which was the first guide dog training centre in the UK.

The selection and training of guide dogs has changed very little since those early days. Before a dog is selected for training it is put through a series of rigorous tests to ensure that it has a stable temperament, that it is not distracted by other dogs, that it reacts favourably in the presence of cats and so on.

As puppies the dogs spend time with puppy walkers who introduce them to the sights, sounds and smells of the world. This involves taking the dogs on buses and trains, into shops and along busy streets. The puppy walker will also teach the puppy to walk ahead on the leash, not 'to heel', as it will once it is a guide dog, and to obey simple commands such as 'sit', 'down', 'stay' and 'come'. Once they commence their full training the dogs learn to walk in a straight line in the centre of the pavement unless there is an obstacle, not to turn corners unless told to do so, to stop at kerbs and wait for the command to cross the road, to turn left or right, to judge height and width so that the owner does not bump their head or shoulder and how to deal with traffic.

In those days, blind people spent four weeks of intensive residential training with their dog, at the end of which the owner handed over a token sum for the animal. Only when the trainer was satisfied that the partnership was working reasonably well were they allowed to return home. Even then it was usually several months before dog and owner became thoroughly adjusted to one another and were working as a single unit.

Today's guide dogs are from well-established breeding lines and tend to be limited to a small number of breeds, the great majority being Labradors and Retrievers. In the early days however, there was a much greater variety in the kinds of dogs used and many were cross-breeds.

My father was paired with Trixie, a Collie cross, and whilst the two of them were training his sister Nip and her husband Howard visited them for a weekend. Whilst they were there Howard fell in love with an Alsatian called Rex which had failed its initial training because it had a habit of chasing cats. He gave the Centre a donation and took Rex home with them on the train.

Once they had completed their training and returned home, my father and Trixie made the daily journey together to Stockton on the Trimdon

Motor Services bus (TMS), where they became very well known amongst the regular passengers. The ultimate aim of guide dog owners is to go unnoticed when they are out and about and not to be given assistance unless it is asked for. The purpose of acquiring a dog is to provide the owner with independence of movement. Nevertheless, there are always times when well-meaning members of the public step in to warn of a ladder in the way or a kerb ahead. This was something my father had to regularly contend with; guide dogs were still not a common sight, especially in Bishop Auckland.

Unfortunately it soon became apparent that Trixie was too small a dog for my father and that she would perhaps be better suited to a lady owner. Reluctantly therefore, she was returned to Leamington to retrain with a new person. My father then had to return to Leamington Spa himself and repeat the process of training with a new dog. This time he was paired with a brindle

Boxer called Major. Once they returned to Bishop Auckland the two of them soon became a familiar sight around the town, my father with his briefcase and trilby hat, Major at his side in his white harness

Bishop Auckland is the principle market town for the Wear Valley area, situated twelve miles south west of Durham City at the point where the River Wear and its tributary the Gaunless converge. It is famous for its football team, The Two Blues, which won the FA Amateur Cup ten times; my mother, whilst pregnant with me, was one of the thousands who travelled to Wembley Stadium in the 1954-55 season to watch them draw with neighbouring Crook. In the middle of the twentieth century Bishop Auckland was thriving. The main thoroughfare was Newgate Street, which follows the line of Roman Dere Street, lined with family-owned shops and businesses and dominated by Doggarts Department Store in the Market Place. The

Market Place in those days held a twice-weekly market which attracted people from all the surrounding villages. It also contains the Town Hall, a grade two listed building in the French Gothic Revival style built in 1862, and the entrance to Auckland Castle, the historical residence of the Prince Bishops of Durham. My father and Major regularly negotiated their way along the length of Newgate Street, he familiar with the names and locations of every crossing they encountered along the way, Major weaving through the crowds of shoppers and skilfully avoiding prams, ladders and any other obstacles.

Major was a very intelligent, gentle-natured dog, although one of his front fangs often stuck outside his lips, which made him look rather fierce – which he wasn't. In fact he must have been extremely patient, as apparently he tolerated my riding round on his back and dressing him up in various outfits. A guide dog will only work when it is in harness, so it can be treated as any other dog when it is not working and my father's dogs were very much family pets as well. All of them had passed the rigorous assessment to be guide dogs, but they each had their own personalities and behaved in slightly different ways when out of harness.

The working relationship between owner and dog takes several months to establish, even after they have returned home. In addition, the family have to make adjustments and get used to having a working dog in their midst. Routine is a very necessary part of the life of a guide dog and its owner. Strict rules have to be adhered to and any temptation to "spoil" the dog has to be resisted. All my father's dogs were kept to a strict diet; in theory no titbits were allowed, and the dogs were only fed once a day, the dog having to sit and wait while the food was placed in front of it and then only eat on command. This was important when it came to those times when my father was away from home on his own and had to feed his dog himself. However, once we all got used to having Major with us he soon proved to be a great asset to my father and a source of reassurance to my mother and the rest of the family.

My father was always smartly dressed, as his appearance was important to him. This was not because of any personal vanity but more about the confidence it gave him, bearing in mind that he could not check his appearance in a mirror. He was always clean shaven and would shave himself using an electric razor. He had dark, curly black hair which he would style using two crocodile hair grips carefully placed to form parallel waves held in place with Brylcreem. He always wore a suit, shirt and tie (tied in a half-Windsor) and an overcoat when appropriate. His only concession to casual wear was a sports jacket and an open-necked shirt and sandals whilst on holiday. We would be his "mirror", checking his shoes were a pair, his socks matched etc, although my mother would always lay out his clothes for him each morning.

My father had a very strong social conscience and was deeply concerned by situations he considered to be unjust or unfair. He was always prepared to speak out or seek ways to rectify a situation and was always concerned about those less fortunate than himself. As a blind person it might have been easy for him to just sit back and let others take care of him, but that was never his way. Having made St Helen's Auckland his adoptive home, he very quickly became involved in the community and set about exploring ways in which he could play an active part within that community.

CHAPTER 5

Working in the community

In 1959 my father was successful in becoming an Independent Councillor on the former Bishop Auckland Urban District Council, representing the St. Helen's Ward. BAUDC was established at the end of the nineteenth century as a result of the 1894 Local Government Act. It was replaced in 1972 by a two-tier District and County System, which meant that Bishop Auckland and the surrounding area were governed by Wear Valley District Council until 2009, when Durham County Council became a Unitary Authority.

In the pamphlet he prepared for the coming election in 1961, he describes himself as: "for no party and against no party, but genuinely anxious to do his best for everyone." He also lists the things he has already been involved with on behalf of both the District as a whole and the people of St. Helen's in particular, such as the improvement of street lighting, the allocation and improvement of council houses, the servicing of roads and drains, the building of garages and the possibility of industrial development. The old-age pensioners and widows of the area had also received monetary gifts at Christmas. He also mentions his endeavour since 1958 to form a Community Association for the people of St. Helen's and Tindale Crescent, which through hard work and perseverance was nearing completion.

The days in the run-up to the election my father, typically, got the entire family involved, pushing leaflets through all the letter boxes in the ward, and Election Day itself was spent driving around St. Helen's with my father speaking through a loudspeaker held out of a car window.

Once re-elected he served on several committees, including those for Housing, Finance and Rates and the South Western Regional Library Advisory Sub-Committee. He liked to tell the story of how one of his first official engagements as a Councillor was to inspect the water and sewerage works on the banks of the River Wear at Binchester, a strange task perhaps for a blind person.

My father's work on the Council meant he had large quantities of papers and reports to deal with, so it was at this time that I began to help by reading these to him. He would make notes in Braille to take with him to the various committee meetings or in order to reply to the many letters he received, and as a result I became quite familiar with what seemed to me at the time the tedious workings of local government.

Once he became an owner of a guide dog himself, my father was passionate about and very involved with the work of the Guide Dogs for the Blind Association and worked hard to raise both funds and awareness. To this end he wrote a Handbook for Voluntary Workers on their behalf in which he gave a brief history of guide dogs, outlined their training, offered advice to new owners, and offered guidelines for the setting up of local fund-raising committees. In it he says: "A guide dog is, in many respects, similar to a motor car— provided the owner knows the way and uses the correct controls, it will take him anywhere."

My father's work for charities, and in particular for the Guide Dogs for the Blind Association, meant that we always seemed to be selling tickets for something; raffles, concerts, cheese and wine parties etc. We collected toiletries and bottles for tombola stalls. We folded thousands of raffle tickets and collected bucketfuls of small change, postage stamps and silver paper. We stood in the streets in all weathers rattling collecting tins on countless flag days. We stood for hours in Bishop Auckland Market Place on Saturday afternoons filling balloons from large bottles of helium gas for balloon races. We attended endless coffee mornings and collected sponsors for everything from silences to walks, all to raise as much money as possible.

As a result of his involvement in charity work my father was frequently invited to attend various functions and fund-raising events, to open fairs and sales of work and to give talks. Inevitably on these occasions it was usually Major who was the star of the show and the fact of my father's blindness would always attract special attention. As a result we were often featured in the local press.

In the early sixties, the radio programme *Down Your Way* visited Bishop Auckland and my father was invited to be one of the local people interviewed on the programme. Following their talk with the presenter, who if my memory is correct was Franklin Engelmann, each of the interviewees was invited to choose a piece of music to be broadcast. It was customary that these musical contributions were from the world of classical music or musical theatre. However, on learning that my father was to appear on the programme I exacted a promise from him that he would ask for my favourite song at the time to be played. So, while his fellow participants chose works from the likes of Mozart and Gershwin, true to his word my father requested they play *My Old Man's a Dustman* by Lonnie Donegan.

The village of St Helen's Auckland is three miles south-west of Bishop Auckland on the A688, which leads to Barnard Castle. Coal was extensively worked in the nineteenth century when there were two collieries. St. Helen's, owned by Joseph Pease & Partners, comprised two pits, namely, the Engine pit and the Tindale pit, and owed its existence to the building of the Darlington and Stockton Railway. The nearby West Auckland Colliery was owned and worked by Bolckow, Vaughan & Co. Ltd.

St Helen's is on the river Gaunless, a tributary of the River Wear. It also lies on the now closed Haggerleases branch railway, once part of the historic Darlington to Stockton Railway, and at the time we lived there it had its own railway station. The church of St. Helen is the most notable building, the oldest part having been built in 1120 AD. It is dedicated to Helen, who was the consort of the Roman Emperor Constantius Chlorus and the mother of Emperor Constantine. Helen had a major influence on her son and as such was an important figure in Christian history.

The only other building of any import is St. Helen's Hall, which is Grade 1 listed, having been built in c1622 for James Carr and extended for William Carr, MP for Newcastle. The frontage to the main road has blind, bricked-up windows giving it a rather mysterious appearance and causing it to be the subject of childhood imaginings of ghosts and hauntings.

St Helen's was a still a small place when we lived there, the area which now contains Tesco, Sainsbury's and other retail outlets being just farmland in those days. Most of the inhabitants were employed locally in the factories on the small trading estate. There were very few if any social facilities, so in the late 1950s my father got together a group of local people to form a Community Association and to raise the money to build a Community Centre. My father had a real gift for getting people involved, his own enthusiasm being infectious and enabling. His family, members of the Committee along with their families and neighbours, all soon found themselves enlisted to collect raffle prizes from local businesses and factories, organise coffee mornings, go door to door collecting for a football sweep, sell tickets for cheese and wine evenings and effectively raise money in whatever way they could. Eventually the Association, with the help of a grant from the County Council, was in a position to buy a piece of land on the trading estate and draw up plans for a community centre building.

My mother and I sat on our living room floor while my father described how he envisaged the single-storey building and we made a floor plan out of Lego bricks so he could feel it. The plan incorporated an entrance hall, toilets, a main hall with a stage, office, lounge, a second minor hall and a kitchen. I think it might be the only building to have been designed out of Lego bricks in this way!

My father laid the foundation stone on the 27th January 1962 and the St. Helen's and Tindale Community Centre was officially opened by Mr D H Curry, Deputy Director of Education for Durham County on Saturday June 23rd 1962. The opening day began at 1pm with a cocktail reception in the home of committee members Ron and Mary Hodgson in Maude Terrace, provided by the builders Messrs D V Roper (Bishop Auckland) Ltd. This was followed by the official opening of the Community Centre at 2pm and a garden fete opened by The Lady Davina Vane.

The Community Centre was used for a variety of functions and soon became the hub of the community. There were youth clubs, old-time dancing, a cycling club, concerts and fairs etc. My mother enjoyed dancing and was a member of the Olde Time Dancing Club, the only leisure time I remember her having. My father on the other hand had little or no sense of rhythm; the only dance he would attempt was the St. Bernard's Waltz, which he would perform stiffly and with great relish—one, two, three, stamp stamp!

As well as taking his place as Chairman of the

Management Committee he would join in with as many of the activities as possible. He especially enjoyed writing the scripts for the frequent community variety shows that were staged and compering them. These gave him the opportunity to exercise his love of writing, often mimicking the popular radio and television shows of the time, but also to employ his rather off-beat sense of humour. In one show the local police sergeant, Fred Humphries, appeared as Englefred Humphreydink. He also compered fashion shows and beauty contests, perhaps not very politically correct these days, reading from his Braille notes and with my mother prompting from the side.

In 1963 the Community Centre became the base for a hospital radio service to Tindale Crescent Hospital, which had begun life as a fever hospital and was at that time providing care for the elderly members of the community. This was run by a small group of volunteers on a Sunday morning and played the patients' musical requests. The

foundation stone has been preserved and incorporated into the fabric of the new building.

Major died very suddenly and unexpectedly of a heart attack whilst we were on holiday. This was a very difficult time for my father. The relationship between a blind person and their guide dog is very close and is built entirely on trust. Major had accompanied my father everywhere and he had absolute and total faith in him, trusting him with his life. The decision to apply for and go forward to train with a new dog was a difficult one. However, without a dog at his side he would have lost the freedom he had become used to and it would have been almost impossible for him to carry out his work, so he returned to Leamington Spa and was retrained with a very large and loveable Yellow Labrador called Shauna.

One of the requirements of being a guide dog is not to be distracted by or aggressive towards other dogs. Shauna however, almost from day one, developed a distinct dislike of a Collie called Rusty which lived a few doors along Simpson Avenue. When in harness she would dutifully ignore Rusty and attend to her work, but out of harness she would chase him at every opportunity.

Similarly, cats should not cause a guide dog any concern. However, for my eleventh birthday I was given a fairly newborn kitten from the nearby farm which we named Thomas. In fairness to Shauna, he was semi-wild and did travail to his bright ginger colouring. However still erratic to Shauna, lashing out with his claws and for the first few days Shauna sported a series of bloody scratch marks on her nose. My mother was reduced to sitting on the bottom of the stairs with Thomas on her lap and Shauna by her side, coaxing and cajoling the two of them to be friends. Eventually peace was restored and the two became almost inseparable.

In April 1961, my brother, David Keith Johnston was born. This of course meant my mother had less time to spend helping my father with his various community involvements, so more responsibility for that gradually fell to me.

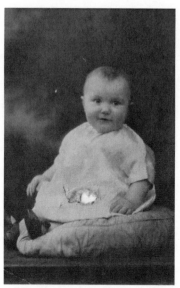

David Ronald Johnston as a baby

With his mother Cordelia before he
lost his sight

With Stan, taken shortly before Stan's death

Wedding at Auckland St Helen Church, August 3rd 1953

With Trixie outside Ashmore's in Stockton

NASCO function, 1958

With Major and his training class at Leamington Spa

Major showing
his tooth

With Major in Newgate Street, Bishop Auckland

Officials and committee members who attended the coffee evening held by the Darlington branch of the Guide Dogs for the Blind Association, at Danby Lodge.—[N.D.]

Guide Dogs for the Blind coffee evening, Danby Lodge, Darlington

**THE URBAN DISTRICT COUNCIL OF
BISHOP AUCKLAND
ELECTION OF TWO COUNCILLORS**
for the
ST. HELEN'S AUCKLAND WARD
on
TUESDAY, 9th MAY, 1961

PRESENTED WITH THE COMPLIMENTS OF

D. R. JOHNSTON

YOUR INDEPENDENT CANDIDATE

WHO IS FOR NO PARTY, AND AGAINST NO PARTY,
BUT GENUINELY ANXIOUS TO DO HIS BEST FOR
EVERYONE.

Election leaflet, Bishop Auckland Urban District Council, 1961

Laying of the foundation stone for St. Helen's and
Tindale Community Centre

Receiving the keys from the builder, Mr Roper

Shauna in the garden at Simpson Avenue

Loading Family Boxes, Oxfam News, January 1966

Dusky in her harness

CHAPTER 6

Oxfam: breaking new ground

In 1963 my father was the successful applicant out of 500 for the position of Regional Organiser for Oxfam, which had been formed as the Oxford Committee for Famine Relief in Oxford in 1942.The group campaigned for food supplies to be sent through an Allied naval blockade to starving women and children in enemy-occupied Greece during the Second World War. In 1951 Leslie Kirkley became General Secretary and over his 24 years at Oxfam he transformed the organisation from a local charity into a world-renowned aid agency. I met Leslie on several occasions when he visited my father's region.

At the time when my father began working for the charity it was still using its original name, and he often came up against people saying they did not know there was a famine in Oxford. As Oxfam and its work was almost unknown in the North of England my father was appointed to raise awareness and set up local committees and fund-raising groups in as many towns as possible. His region covered all of the North East, from the Tweed to the Humber and what was then Cumberland. This meant a lot of travelling for him and Shauna, using public transport. On evenings, weekends and during the school holidays I often would go with him on these trips.

We made many an arduous journey to places like Workington and Millom over Bowes Moor and to Consett and Stockton, always on the bus. My role was to make sure my father arrived on time, to describe the venues we went to and be his eyes in the countless meetings he arranged. I would sit beside him at a table at the front and before the meeting started I would describe the room – where the doors and windows were, how the chairs were arranged, how many people were present and where particular people were sitting – Mrs. Brown is at three o'clock, Mr. Smith at ten o'clock etc. My father had an amazing capacity to remember people by the sound of their voices. However, if someone spoke in the meeting whose voice he didn't recognise I would describe the speaker to him – an elderly lady with grey hair and glasses, a young man with long hair and a beard etc.

At times these occasions must have been very frustrating for him. Well-meaning people had a tendency to talk to me instead of directly to him: 'Does your Dad want a cup of tea?' 'Does he take sugar?' 'Is your Dad comfortable sitting there?' and so on. I think I just went along with this at first, but I soon learned to politely suggest they should ask him themselves.

At first my father had his office in our spare bedroom in Simpson Avenue and my mother acted as his unpaid secretary. Gradually I took over the task of reading to him the large amount of post that arrived every day and the minutes from all those meetings while my father made notes in Braille. My father had a wooden channel fastened to the front of his desk through which he would feed the paper from the shorthand machine to read it and then type his letters etc using a conventional typewriter which had a Braille guide added.

Many people have spoken of my father's gift of inspiring and encouraging those he worked alongside. One such person was a young man called David Browning, who was a volunteer member of the Oxfam Group my father established in Blythe, Northumberland. My father invited and encouraged him to be the representative of the Northern Region on Oxfam's Council of Management. On rather nervously accepting the role David was capitulated into a realm of work and programmes of meetings and although still only in his twenties he was able to make contributions on the Council from a North-Eastern perspective. David went on to become Oxfam's first Staff Development Manager in the voluntary sector and to work with Oxfam worldwide developing training and learning on development issues. He recalls that my father's insight in nominating him for the role on the Council was a decisive moment in his life; my father he says "was the sponsor of the particular direction in which the rest of my life was to travel".

As the administrative work increased my father soon required qualified help and so he engaged Jean Anderton as his part-time secretary, whom he had come to know through her role as Secretary to the Community Association. She recalls that working with my father soon became full time and then time and a half. Jean worked for my father for the next four years until the birth of her first child. She was very shy at first, but as a result of the trust my father had in her capabilities her confidence increased to the extent that she was soon working as his assistant.

Jean was herself a qualified typist and never ceased to marvel at the accuracy of my father's typing and the attention to detail he showed in whatever he undertook. He was a perfectionist and nothing left his office with even the smallest of mistakes. Jean was never tempted not to inform him of her own mistakes as she respected the standards he set himself. My father's sight loss was never an issue in their working relationship; on the contrary, Jean always looked to him for guidance and learned much from him.

Eventually working from the confines of a small spare bedroom became difficult and impracticable, so my father moved into offices in Victoria Street in Bishop Auckland, above what was then a music shop called Brotherton's. My father liked to come home for his lunch each day. Although he had every faith in Shauna's ability the road at that time of day was very busy, so I would come out of school, cross over the road with Mrs. Shaw, the lollipop lady, and walk down the village to the bus stop outside the factories to meet him off Stephenson's bus at quarter past twelve and take him over the road. I was often in trouble for being late, as I would dawdle and daydream on the way; I was still only nine or ten at this time. It's strange when I look back that I was trusted to cross him over the road but not allowed to cross the same road when I was on my own!

The loss of the sense of sight means a person has to develop other ways of keeping in touch with the world around them. My father had many ways of maintaining this contact. He was always thankful for and protective of his hearing, which was precious to him, always maintaining that being without sight was far less isolating than being without hearing. He wore a watch, the face of which was hinged, allowing him to open it and read the Braille dial. His Roberts radio was a real asset to him, providing him with news and entertainment. As a family we would occasionally watch television together, but as so much relied on the visual it usually meant one of us providing an additional commentary for my father. In fact in later years the television was in our front lounge, and only really used when we had company and when Ian and I were courting. Instead we listened to the radio, where my father was at no disadvantage. I have fond memories of my younger years and our listening together to what was then the Light Programme, to programmes including *Does the Team Think* with regular panellists

Jimmy Edwards, Arthur Askey and Ted Ray, *The Clitheroe Kid* and *The Navy Lark*.

The radio also provided my father with a means of keeping up to date with local, national and international events by means of the news broadcasts and current affairs programmes. An exception was made on the night of 21st/22nd July 1969 when my father sat in front of our small black and white television set and "watched" the BBC television coverage of the first moon landings by Neil Armstrong and Buzz Aldrin. The fact that the pictures were faint and grainy was of no consequence to him of course, as he listened to James Burke's voice describe what others were trying to assimilate with their eyes.

My father was a big fan of sport, particularly of cricket, football and boxing. Cricket, and in particular the Test Match, would provide the backdrop to our summers. He would sit in the garden on fine days with his radio at his feet tuned to the Third Programme and Test Match

Special with the voice of John Arlott giving a ball-by-ball commentary. He was also a Newcastle United fan and his radio would give him access to commentaries on all their big games. I am in no doubt that my father could "see" all the action of the game when listening to the commentary. Likewise he would become totally involved in the drama of the big boxing bouts of the day, especially heavyweights like Joe Frazier, George Foreman and of course Mohammed Ali, often listening through the night.

The Grand National was another favourite, the only occasion on which my mother would place a bet, and the household had to maintain absolute silence as my father earnestly listened to stride-by-stride accounts of the race, with every jump and every fall.

To this day I still prefer to have the radio playing when I am in the house on my own and my brother, who is also a sports fan, still prefers to listen to cricket on the radio.

But it was his sense of touch that provided my father with a way of "seeing" the world around him. His fingers were particularly sensitive and he would use them with great dexterity to familiarise himself with where things were and what they looked like. This sometimes called for a certain amount of patience on our part as it meant that some things would take longer, and doing anything spontaneously was out of the question. Any outing, visit or family event had to be talked about and organised in advance. New household items, clothes, etc would be very carefully examined. If we were attending a special occasion our outfits would also receive the same careful scrutiny. Sadly my father died before Ian and I were married, but I have the poignant memory of Charles before we left for the church emotionally saying he could just see my father carefully examining my dress and veil and smelling my bouquet.

As a family we enjoyed playing games

together, our favourites being cards, dominoes and Scrabble. We played with Braille versions of all of these. The playing cards had Braille in the top right-hand corner, the dominoes had raised dots and the Scrabble board had a raised grid into which the tiles could fit, each tile having a Braille letter embossed on it. Our favourite card games were Rummy, Black Horse and Newmarket. If we played on a Sunday evening however we would play with buttons instead of pennies as stakes, as my Granda Harrie would not allow gambling on a Sunday. My father excelled at all of these games, mostly due to the fact that he had an exceptional memory and a very logical brain. He would memorise the dominoes that had been laid and calculate who was holding what. He remembered which cards had been played and by whom, and had an extensive vocabulary when it came to Scrabble. Trying to cheat against him was out of the question.

We would also play games of cricket, usually

on the beach, with a rubber ball which had large holes in it and a bell inside allowing my father to hear it coming. The bowler would shout "bowl!" before bowling underarm to him. Invariably the other occupants of the beach would take an interest and end up joining in the game.

Like all blind people, my father's lack of sight meant he had an increased awareness of danger; he sensed it all around us. At home lights had to be turned off when no one was in the room, electrical items unplugged when not in use, pans never left unattended on the stove, the fireguard always in place. Roads were a particular danger. No one in our street had a car in those days and the only traffic on the street was usually the bin wagon once a week – the postman had a bike, Mrs Sanderson delivered the milk from a hand cart, the rag and bone man had a horse and cart. Even so, to my father the dangers of the road were an ever-present reality and he instilled in us the need always to be careful when we were near to or crossing a road. The main road through St Helen's however is the A688 and it is and was even then a busy road. In addition, when the factories turned out at five o'clock, the traffic increased many times. Therefore, unlike my friends, I was not allowed to cross the road on my own in order to play in the fields behind the factories. This caused me some resentment at times, as I would be left alone when the others had gone over the road to play. I never broke the rule however, although I suspect my brother David did.

Water was another perceived danger to my father. We were never allowed to play unsupervised beside any water. When my mother took us for a picnic beside the River Gaunless, which runs through St. Helen's on its way to join the River Wear in Bishop Auckland, he would become anxious, although it is not much more than a stream. He would repeatedly remind us of the dangers before we went and I suspect he did not rest until we arrived safely home again.

There was also a particularly deep pond in the fields near Woodhouses, the remains of old mine workings, as there was a pit heap nearby where we sometimes played. My father had a deep fear of this pond, although I suspect he had never been near it. In his mind's eye though it represented a great threat, and he would absolutely forbid me to go anywhere near it, relating tales of children drowning in such ponds. As a result I too became terrified of the weed-covered pond, where I imagined terrible water creatures lived just waiting to lure unsuspecting girls like me into its watery depths.

Probably the greatest threat to our safety though was Bonfire Night. We would always have a small bonfire in the garden with a homemade guy on the top and my mother would buy a box of Standard fireworks. The whole occasion was fraught with danger. We had to stand a safe distance away from the fire and only my mother was allowed anywhere near the fireworks, as it was these that most troubled my father. They had to be transferred into an old biscuit tin and my mother had to follow the instructions exactly. There was no going back to a firework if it did not go off, which was quite often in those days. They were all quite pathetic compared to the ones available today, usually just fizzing for a second or two and occasionally spitting out a few coloured sparks. Bangers were not allowed, the unpredictability of Jumping Jacks made them a particular hazard and we were always reminded that Catherine Wheels had the potential to spin off the fence post. As a consequence I was terrified of them all. My favourites were the sparklers, but even with them great caution had to be taken, so much so that any enjoyment was somewhat tempered. Like all my friends I would excitedly look forward to Bonfire Night for weeks beforehand, but when the night actually arrived it was always filled with tension and fear.

We were luckier than many of the children who

lived around us when it came to Christmas. We were not well off by any means, but our parents always managed to buy us a number of presents, although not on the scale of today's children, and we had generous family members. Christmas Day was always one of order and routine; never the mad scramble to open presents in the early hours of the morning in our house. On Christmas Eve we would hang our pillow cases on the drawers of the sideboard in the living room. My mother would be first up on Christmas morning and would go downstairs first – when we were younger, it was to check if Santa had been– and light the coal fire in the living room. We would all get washed and dressed and then sit down at the kitchen table and have breakfast, after which my mother would wash up. The door to the living room remained firmly closed. My father would then have a shave and go to the toilet while my mother took the dog out. Our friends by this time had been up for hours and had opened all their presents, and were often bewildered that we were still waiting to open ours.

Only when all was ready could we all go into the living room together. There would be a pile of presents for each of us and we would sit beside ours and take turns to open one. The label had to be read aloud for my father and then the present itself passed to him for examination before the process was repeated with the next person. Opening everyone's presents took a considerable time! I think I always understood the need to have order and discipline so as to allow my father to participate, but in retrospect I sense that maybe some of the excitement was lost.

My father loved reading. Every couple of weeks my mother or I would read the catalogue which came from the RNIB Library Service to him and he would choose and order library books. These would arrive by mail in large, sturdy brown boxes. There were usually several volumes to each book, which were each approximately A3 in size and were hard backed with thick brown paper pages. My father would read the Braille with two hands, the book balanced on his knees. His brother Cliff always blamed the fact that he was a poor sleeper on his having to share a bed with Dad as a boy and my father keeping him awake by reading in bed.

My father would also read bedtime stories to us. These were from less cumbersome books, soft backed and pale blue, no pictures of course. I had two favourites; St. John's Gospel and the Milly Molly Mandy stories by Joyce Lankester Brisley. Looking back I wonder if these influenced in any way the callings I felt in life; primary school teaching, library work and ordained ministry.

Throughout his life my father loved the written word. Whether through letters, reports, speeches, lectures or simply for pleasure, he enjoyed the craft of writing. In the early 1950s he wrote a semi-autobiographical novel entitled "Left Hand Down a Bit" which was a catchphrase from *The Navy Lark*, one of his favourite radio programmes, as well as being an oblique reference to working a guide dog. It was never published and sadly has not survived.

He also enjoyed writing poetry, but again very little has survived as his poems were typed on flimsy typing paper. Many of his poems reflected his own experience of being blind, as in "Dreams", whereas others expressed his concern with social justice and fairness. Two such poems have survived:

The Cruel Hand

Behold a cat upon a wall;
An urchin's hand; a fearsome fall.
And who can tell what bitter pain
Is surging through that feline brain!

Behold an urchin in a street;
A sudden punch; he's off his feet.
"You coward, you!" the urchin cries,
I'll burst your nose and black your eyes!"

Behold a cat upon a wall;
An urchin's hand; a fearsome fall.
What torture fills that feline brain!
But what revenge can he obtain!

The Silent Witness

In the midst of London's din,
Where the depths of deadly sin
Mingle freely with the good;
'Mid the traffic's hectic hum
With her feet and fingers numb,
Patiently the Orphan stood.

In the throes of friendless fear,
Bravely bearing every sneer,
Silently she waited there.
Though her face was drawn with pain,
Though her eyes reflected strain,
No kind soul assisted her.

'Mid the throngs of Leicester Square,
Grasping feebly at the air,
Suddenly the Orphan fell.
In the dark and chilly gloom
Of a wretched workhouse room,
Friendlessly she quit this hell.

In the seething surge of life,
Where the selfish streak is rife,
Not a single heart was grieved.
No one felt the need to mourn
O'er a pauper, bastard-born!
Charity was much relieved!

My father had an incredible general knowledge;
his memory was encyclopaedic, despite not having
the advantage of being able to consult the likes of
an atlas, history book or scientific manual.
Information relating to literature, geography,
history, science and politics was all stored in his
head and retrieved with ease. He also possessed

remarkable problem-solving skills and the capability to address and resolve any situation which presented itself by somehow visualising it in his head. This was particularly apparent when he was involved in organising events or campaigns, when he would have a clear picture in his mind of the desired outcomes as well as the details of what was needed in order to achieve them. In this respect his organisational skills were quite outstanding. Alongside this he had a natural and contagious enthusiasm which enabled and carried along all those with whom he came into contact.

CHAPTER 7

Life and work
with my father

My maternal grandparents, Harrie and Connie, were both rather small in stature; Connie was probably only five feet tall, whereas my father's mother, Cordelia, was somewhat taller. To distinguish between them I called them Big Gran and Little Gran. When my Grandfather Harrie retired from the grocery trade they moved into a council bungalow in Dalton Close, just a few hundred yards from our house. They were both still involved with St Helen's church; Harrie was Churchwarden and Connie played the organ.

My grandfather was a very serious sort of man. He had served with the Durham Light Infantry during the First World War and had been taken prisoner and treated badly – I believe he was pushed down a stone staircase – and consequently walked with a limp. He rarely smiled but was a lovely, gentle man.

Little Gran was a very good pianist and gave piano lessons to local children. I must have been a great disappointment to her as my musical ability is nil, although I am sure she would have been pleased to know that my daughter Heather has inherited her musical genes.

Every Sunday afternoon we would go to Little Gran's and sometimes when tea was finished she would play the piano for us. Occasionally my father would entertain us too. He had many gifts, but music was not one of them; like many in our family he was tone deaf. This did not stop him though. He would take his seat at the piano, place his foot firmly on the loud pedal and thump out the music hall song "She was sweet sixteen, little Angeline, always dancing on the village green." I don't remember him playing anything else and on reflection I am not sure it was entirely appropriate for genteel Sunday entertainment. It must have been excruciating for Little Gran, but I thought it was marvellous. It has come as rather a surprise, as I am sure it would have been to my Little Gran, to learn that he studied the piano at Benwell and achieved Grade 3.

Our family holidays were usually taken in Hartlepool, and when I look back getting there was something resembling a military operation. We would travel on the TMS bus from Bishop Auckland market place; my parents, David, me, Shauna, Shauna's harness, Shauna's bed,

Shauna's food, several volumes of my father's Braille books which were big heavy things in canvas cases, my father's Braille machine as well as our cases. What a sight we must have been!

My father would entertain us all with stories from his childhood in Hartlepool. He particularly loved to tell one about when his father Stan was still alive and owned several cars which he kept in a garage near the Fish Sands. My father loved to sit in the driver's seat and pretend to drive while Stan washed the car. One day when he was about eight he released the handbrake and the car he was in ran down the road, through the archway in the sea wall and onto the Fish Sands. The sight of a blind boy driving a car must have given the holiday makers quite a turn!

We would always spend part of our holiday fishing. I particularly remember one August Bank Holiday Monday when we were fishing off the end of the pier with our hand lines. My father was parked beside the wall out of the wind reading one of his Braille books with Shauna quietly sleeping at his side. Suddenly there was a loud cry from one of our fellow fishermen further down the pier and quite a commotion. Apparently as the fisherman had cast his rod and line, Shauna had grabbed the bait and swallowed it – hook, line and sinker! My mother had to find a local vet who was willing to open on Bank Holiday Monday and then get us all there so the offending article could be removed.

At the age of eleven I moved from St Helen's Auckland Junior School to King James 1st Grammar School in Bishop Auckland. In my first year one of the subjects I studied was physics, not one of my best. The school had just moved to a new curriculum, Nuffield Physics, and unfortunately the textbooks had arrived but none of the practical equipment. So for the first term we did nothing in lesson time and the teacher would set us a couple of questions from the text book as homework. Bearing in mind that the problems were intended to be solved using the practical apparatus which was missing, this was a bit of a challenge. My best friend Susan's dad was a teacher at a nearby school and he would take her questions into his school for the physics teacher there to work out. However, my father came to my rescue. It would perhaps take him all week but he would work out the answers in his head!

It was shortly after starting at the grammar school that I became aware for the first time that to other people my father was thought of as disabled. Fifty years on, I can clearly remember the day it happened. In our English Language class at school we were encouraged to have pen pals in America, so I wrote to Patti Yoder in Pennsylvania telling her all about myself and my family. It was a Saturday morning when her reply came and I read it at the table over breakfast. I clearly remember saying to my mother – "Patti says she is very sorry to hear about my Dad, what does she mean?" Life with my father was just normal for me.

Life with my father meant simple things, like not going into a room without making a noise, and speaking to him straight away if he came into the room so he would know someone was there. It meant telling him where the meat, potatoes etc, were on his plate, not changing any of the furniture around so he could safely move around the house and not leaving things lying on the floor or on the stairs. It meant observing the people and things around us and then describing them to him. None of these things felt at all unusual to me.

As far as I was concerned my father was the most able person I knew, and have known; he just couldn't see. So Patti's comment was somewhat bewildering; I felt we did not warrant her pity. I think our pen-pal relationship was quite short lived!

A major part of my father's job was to open the first Oxfam shops in the North and establish groups of local volunteers to run them. Although the first permanent Oxfam Gift Shop had opened on Broad Street in Oxford in 1947, my father began his task by negotiating the temporary use of empty shops. He established committees and shops in twenty-one different towns across his region. When a shop became available in a particular town my mother and I would often go with him in order to describe what it looked like, the condition it was in, its position on the high street and the other shops around it, how big the windows were etc. We would pace out the size of the shop floor with him and check if there was a bus stop nearby. My mother also took on the role of overseeing the shops in Bishop Auckland, sorting, pricing and displaying the donated goods as well as arranging the rotas for the volunteers. Over the years there were several different shops in Newgate Street. I would help by serving on Saturdays and during the school holidays. I learned from my mother how to sort and price clothes and bric a brac and became quite expert at window displays.

In 1964 Oxfam Activities was launched and

Oxfam shops started selling handicrafts and Christmas cards made in developing countries, giving small-scale producers fair prices, training, advice and funding. This was the beginning of what we would later come to know as Fair Trade. I was intrigued by what appeared to my eyes exotic goods which were for sale. Some of the early items which I remember buying were a tea towel printed with "Sita", an Indian doll to cut out and sew and a set of metal wind chimes with strange foreign writing and symbols painted in red on them.

In 1963 the Disasters Emergency Committee (DEC) was formed in the wake of the Skopje earthquake disaster in the former Yugoslavia, consisting of Oxfam, the British Red Cross, Christian Aid and War on Want. Later in his career my father would attend these meetings when international disasters occurred. He had a small staff by this time; an assistant called Jim Agar, his secretary Jean Anderton and a clerk, Janice Clark. They were all were loyal and accepted the challenges and the inevitable extra work that came from having a boss who was blind. Jean and Janice have both remained family friends.

There was still always plenty for me to do, however. I would go into the office with my father on Saturday mornings and read his post so he could catch up, always making copious notes. Several times a year there would be national campaigns to raise money, often during a major famine or other such emergency. At these times I was called in to fold letters and leaflets and put them into envelopes to be posted out. I must have folded thousands of leaflets over the years. In the early 1960s a scheme of 'Pledge Giving' was introduced whereby collectors asked neighbours and friends to give a shilling a month and in return a monthly newsletter would be sent out— more folding and putting into envelopes!

A major campaign in 1966 was the Family Box Campaign, whereby thousands of little cardboard boxes with slits in the top were sent out for people to put their small change in. The winter of 1966 was one of the worst on record, especially in the North East. The campaign was launched at the end of November in the midst of chest-high snowdrifts. My father's assistant, Jim Agar, battled through blizzards and icy roads throughout November and December to deliver boxes to almost 200 distribution points in Northumberland, Durham, Cumberland and Westmorland. Despite the horrendous conditions, all the Family Boxes were distributed with the help of thousands of volunteers.

My father received a call from the press asking if they could take a photograph to accompany an article about the campaign. It was quite late in the evening as I remember and we had to don layers of warm clothing and trek through the snow to the Community Centre to have our photograph taken with the then St. Helen's Community Queen.

1966 was also the year when there were severe floods in India and in response Oxfam supported a growing number of sponsored walks. These were usually run in conjunction with local youth groups and sometimes took place during the night and stations were set up along the route where participants were supplied with food and water. My father took an active interest in these events, always having a clear vision in his head of what was to take place and providing clear and ordered instructions to volunteers. He would often go out during the night to visit those manning the stations and to encourage the walkers. Large amounts of money were raised in this way; in 1966 sponsored walks nationally raised £50,000. However tragedy struck at the start of one of the walks when a crowd of walkers surged against a gate, resulting in a young girl losing her life. Although my father was not involved directly, he felt a strong sense of responsibility and it took him a long time to come to terms with it. Following this mass starts were banned and my father's enthusiasm for this form of fund-raising waned.

1967 saw the start of the Nigerian Civil war, better known perhaps as the Biafran War, a conflict which was fought around political, economic, ethnic, cultural and religious tensions. By 1968 the Federal Military Government had imposed a blockade which led to severe famine. Over the two and a half years that the war lasted an estimated two million people died from starvation and disease. For the first time graphic images of starving children were seen nightly on television reports and people all around the world demanded action.

Frederick Forsyth famously wrote: "Quite suddenly we'd touched a nerve. Nobody in this country at that time had ever seen children looking like that. The last time the Brits had seen anything like that must have been the Belsen pictures... people who couldn't fathom the political complexities of the war could easily grasp the wrong in a picture of a child dying of starvation."

Leslie Kirkley was moved to launch an appeal for emergency funds to help those in Biafra. This was one of Oxfam's first field operations and helped to turn the organisation into a household name. The operation was not without controversy, the Biafran government being accused of running a propaganda campaign and Oxfam, along with other agencies, later admitted to errors of judgement. As a result it made significant changes to its operational methods on the ground. However the relief of the suffering of those involved was a priority; Reverend Nicholas Stacey, Deputy Director of Oxfam at the time, was reported as saying in *The Spectator* on 11th July 1968: "...all Oxfam advertisements, broadcasts and articles have made it abundantly clear that our main immediate concern is for the Ibos in beleaguered Biafra, simply because in terms of human suffering they are in the greatest need."

My father passionately motivated his volunteers, groups, committees, churches, schools, civic heads, newspapers and individuals to get involved with fund-raising efforts, referring to this initial stage of the campaign as a "general mobilisation". His Regional Office in Bishop Auckland co-ordinated house-to-house collections and a leaflet entitled "Emergency Express" was circulated in towns and cities throughout the North East. The Mayor of Sunderland agreed to support the local Oxfam Committee's activities, while the Mayor of Hartlepool selected Oxfam as one of his charities of the year and donated the proceeds of a Floral Ball. The Chairman of Maryport UDC promised to support Oxfam during his term of office, appeal letters appeared in most local newspapers, and coffee mornings and sponsored walks were organised.

My father encouraged all Oxfam supporters to write to their local MP urging them to pressurise the government regarding free access to Biafra for relief organisations and also about bringing about a ceasefire. In an appeal encouraging supporters to continue their efforts, he wrote on the 26th June 1968 in the *Oxfam Actuator*, an information sheet he personally prepared and typed and which was sent out in times of special need with the purpose of evoking action: "These next ten days are going to be very critical ones, for it must be during this period that the dreadful situation comes fully to light – largely engineered by Oxfam. It is not an overstatement to say that all of us in the Organisation are closely involved participants in a dramatic moment of modern history."

He reported that 185 schools had distributed leaflets on the streets and to houses throughout the North and 1,000 individuals had been invited to organise fund-raising events. The Bishop of Newcastle, The Rt Reverend Hugh Ashdown, had urged his Diocesan Conference to support Oxfam's Biafra Emergency Fund and had sent personal letters on the subject to 260 clergy in the diocese. Other Anglican and Catholic Bishops had been urged to do likewise. The Area Secretaries of many social and service organisations had been requested to enlist the help of their branches and appeal letters sent to 45 newspapers in the Region, with five being asked to give special coverage of the emergency.

On the 3rd of July my father reported that donations and offers of help were increasing with every post and that the Bishop of Durham, the Rt. Reverend Ian Ramsay, had written: "I am sure we will not ignore this urgent matter". Haltwhistle, Heaton and Windermere Oxfam Committees were organising special efforts; Jesmond and Kendal were asking local churches and organisations to promote fund-raising events. Wigton had arranged a collection in a local factory and Cockermouth Grammar School was having a series of events. The Chairmen of Seaton Valley and Stanley Urban District Councils had sent donations and the Mayors of Carlisle, Teesside and Workington were considering doing so.

The Lord Mayor of Newcastle had agreed to

open a Special Appeal, with the launch taking place in the Guild Hall on Thursday 18th July. Representatives from churches, local organisations and large companies were invited to attend and were given details of the emergency and asked to arrange fund-raising events. The Mayor of Gateshead was considering making a similar appeal. A city-wide house-to-house collection was organised in Newcastle and a Donor's Coupon had appeared in *The Journal*, the editor of which had promised strong publicity backing all Oxfam's efforts. Several people had received encouraging personal letters from their MPs.

My father continued to rally his volunteers and committees, and wrote: "This is the way to do it! Get everybody involved. Get the whole town working for the children of Biafra." The *Oxfam Actuator* in July also included information from a recent report from Father Byrne, a Catholic missionary working in Biafra, which described how Oxfam funds had been used to evacuate thousands of refugees from war-torn areas. Father Byrne was quoted as saying: "I doubt if any grant has been used as effectively as this one in saving thousands of lives. I wish the people of Oxfam could see some of these refugees. I interviewed many of them. But for the transportation supplied by Oxfam's grant, these people would almost certainly have died. They had walked from Sukka and took up residence in Udi (200 miles). Then lorries met them when they were exhausted from fatigue and hunger. One girl was found struggling along carrying her crippled father on her back."

Leslie Kirkley had recently returned from a visit to Biafra and reported that the famine was "amongst the worst I have seen". He had appealed to the British Government to allow the RAF to fly in supplies from Fernando Po and said that the 600,000 people in hastily-organised refugee camps were undoubtedly better off than the three to four million outside the camps. He was quoted as saying "a catastrophic situation probably beyond any scale hitherto will develop in six weeks if supplies into Biafra are not dramatically stepped up". The Oxfam Actuator dated July 14th began with the statement: "There will be no let-up in Oxfam's appeal. The need exists and sooner or later it must be met."

To that end volunteers were encouraged to raise as much money as possible in readiness for a massive relief operation immediately free access was obtained. The blockade was being beaten wherever possible and refugees on the Federal side of the firing lines being helped. Fund-raising events in my father's Region were continuing apace. The Bishop of Hexham and Newcastle, the Rt Reverend James Cunningham, was to commend Oxfam's Emergency Fund in his next letter to Catholic clergy. The Chairmen of Bishop Auckland, Easington and Millom councils were writing to over 100 churches and organisations in their Districts inviting them to arrange fund-raising events or send donations and Emergency Express was now circulating in almost the whole of the Region. The local Oxfam Committees were hard at work; Cramlington were writing to schools and factories, Gosforth were holding coffee mornings and planning a flag day, Maryport were having a coffee day, Sunderland had held a collection at the Air Show, Carlisle were organising a city wide event. My father further encouraged all the Committees to consider seeking permission to hold collections at organised events such as agricultural shows, race meetings, cricket matches and gymkhanas, as well as in pubs and clubs, lidos, country houses open to the public, foyers of cinemas and bingo halls and factory entrances. Special fund-raising materials such as posters, car stickers and fliers were available from the Bishop Auckland office.

CHAPTER 8

The pressures increase

As well as being involved in the fund-raising efforts of Oxfam, my father played a great part in the work of breaking down people's prejudices and misconceptions of the work it undertook, with such ideas as the commonly-held belief that charity should begin at home, that such work was the concern of governments, concerns about administration costs and rotting food on quaysides, birth control etc. He worked tirelessly to bring the truth and reality to people in ways they could understand. All of this was fuelled by his own strongly-held beliefs and reinforced by his own personal experience. His reason for helping the poorer parts of the world was simply that it was right. A poor world was an insecure one, and that affected us all. In the 1970s he wrote of a world "still divided by nationalism, self-interest, prejudice and fear. These are the real barriers to the elimination of hunger, poverty, pollution, violence and other human ills. Only when people learn to love the world as much as they love their own countries will there be any hope of true peace and justice on earth."

The day-to-day work of promoting Oxfam's work in the Region continued and information and support continued to flow from the Regional Office. Strong recommendations were made at a Regional Conference that permanent shops should be established in towns where there was an Oxfam Committee and where premises and helpers could be obtained. It was recommended that every Committee should have a Pledge Gifts Group Collector and a Promoter, and there was unanimous agreement that Young Oxfam Groups should be based in educational establishments and youth clubs.

The purchase of a vehicle to house a mobile exhibition, project films and recruit supporters was under consideration. My father felt the running costs of such a vehicle could be justified but was hesitant about using funds to purchase it. He came up with a scheme whereby 5000 books of Green Shield Stamps cashed at a special rate allowed to Oxfam of 15 shillings a book would produce the estimated cost of purchasing and equipping a Land Rover and specially-tailored trailer. Everyone therefore was urged to get people collecting Green Shield Stamps and to send the completed books to his office (no prizes for guessing whose task it was to count them!) He also realised that filling stations had quantities of unclaimed stamps, so he urged volunteers to approach local proprietors in their areas.

By this time the work my father was doing to raise Oxfam's profile in the North was coming more and more to the attention of those in Oxfam House. In 1969 Leslie Kirkley suggested that my parents might visit some of Oxfam's overseas projects. In considering this my father, with typical humility, felt it would be more beneficial, and less costly, if he became involved in a short-term overseas assignment which would offer him an opportunity to use his particular talents. He suggested that perhaps a newsworthy way of launching Oxfam's Wider Role Campaign might be for him to deliver a charter to U Thant, Secretary General of the United Nations (1961-1971), followed by a press conference, and then deliver copies to government officials in various capital cities.

In his reply to Leslie, in a very poignant and personal letter dated 15th June, my father refers to his blindness and the inevitability of the media and press focusing on that in any such assignment. He stresses his concerns that any such assignment should not be seen as a stunt or gimmick. Instead he suggests that his "so-called disability" could be used to some advantage. He points out that the situation of the developing countries was in some ways similar to the experiences he had himself had to face. Like them he had had to contend with prejudice, misconceptions and mistrust. Although he was well qualified both professionally and personally and more than able to compete on equals terms with his sighted colleagues, those in positions of power and authority had not had the will or the courage to allow him to prove his worth within society or the economy. He, and others in the same position, had always been seen as second class, as not having anything to offer in their own right.

In his own words: "Then suddenly, when there seemed to be no hope of ever making a breakthrough, Oxfam gave me a chance." The right opportunity for my father to make an overseas trip does not appear to have presented itself, although my father's fear of overseas travel, and in particular water, may well have been a contributing factor.

My father's loyalty to Oxfam was total and his dedication and commitment to their cause absolute. This did not prevent him from being forthright in voicing his concerns and putting forward positive suggestions for ways to improve the efficiency and effectiveness of their work however. With the help of archivist Antonia White, I have come across a paper co-written by my father and his colleague Peter Briggs dated 20th November 1972 entitled "Two Men's Thoughts on Regional Management". In it they express their concerns over the stresses and strains which Oxfam's management system at that time placed upon those involved in it. This, they point out, was a direct result of the organisation's growth. They go on to list some of the main factors which were "militating against success" and then try to devise ways of eliminating them. They also outline a suggestion for a complete reordering of the managerial structures of the organisation. There is perhaps some irony that these concerns were highlighted a mere four years before my father suffered a breakdown as a result of stress and overworking, which would lead to an illness which brought about his untimely death.

My father's position meant he was entitled to a car and so, although she was then in her forties, my mother learned to drive. The first car we had was a green Morris 1000 estate car, a "woodie" (with a wood-framed body). Dad was thrilled with it and I had the task of reading the manual to him whilst he absorbed and memorised all the facts and figures. It was the same with all the cars we had. His love of cars was probably inherited from Stan, and the one regret he had was that he was not able to drive. He did experience driving however, as he occasionally persuaded Charles to sit in with him and be his eyes while he drove around the trading estate.

The loss of one of the senses has the effect of heightening the others. My father had very good hearing, an exceptional sense of touch and a strong sense of direction and spatial awareness. The latter was often the cause of some heated discussion between him and me when we were travelling. He would be seated in the front passenger seat while I was in the back with the road atlas and in charge of navigation. Sadly my own sense of direction is not so good, nor is my ability to determine right from left. As a result I would direct my mother in one direction, only for my father to shout "not that way, we'll end up in the sea!" or some such comment. This would continue for most of the journey, with me frantically turning the map this way and that and my father constantly putting me right. In the meantime my mother would calmly drive on and get us to our destination without our help.

In 1970 my father was promoted to being Northern Director of Oxfam, a position which brought more responsibility and work for him. We also moved house at this time; 3 Rosemount Road, South Church was the first house my parents had owned. It was a large, four-bedroomed, double-fronted end terrace with a garden and garage. Situated at the crest of the bank on the road leading to Shildon, it commanded good views of the church, the bridge across the river and what was left of the village. My father was thrilled with it. Of course it brought extra work for my mother, but she embraced this with her usual fortitude and found great pleasure in decorating, carpeting and furnishing the house and redesigning the garden. It was a special house for me also; it somehow seemed to represent all my parents had achieved against the odds.

The ancient village of South Church is situated on the River Gaunless, where the river is crossed by a single-arched stone bridge. The village is dominated by St. Andrew's, the largest parish church in the Diocese of Durham, probably of Anglo Saxon origin, and nearby is the 13th Century building which once housed the College of Priests, the oldest occupied building in County Durham.

In the 19th Century the coming of railways and coalmining brought industrial growth and the village was surrounded by pits and drifts. However, as the coal and railways industries declined the houses became little more than slums; low and two-storeyed with only two or three rooms arranged close together around courtyards with unmade roads.

By the time we arrived in 1971 much of this had been cleared, although derelict buildings, the remains of a mill, still stood in the area in front of the church, along with one terrace where a few families still lived. New houses had been built close to the river and these were in constant threat of flooding. There were two pubs; the Red Alligator, named after a horse trained in Bishop Auckland by Denys Smith which won the Grand National in 1968, and the Coach and Horses, a Post Office, a shop, the Working Men's Club and a Methodist chapel. Perhaps my ecumenical tendencies began here as I would attend Morning Communion at St. Andrew's with my mother and then slip down the bank and into the back of the chapel in the evening.

My father, armed as he was with a huge sense of community, was keen to engage in village life, and he decided the best place to start was to have a pint in the Working Men's Club. So one Friday night I reluctantly linked his arm and we walked, innocent as lambs, down the bank, across the bridge and into the club. I dutifully opened the door to the main room, which was swirling with cigarette smoke and about half full of men all holding pint glasses. The effect was instant—absolute silence fell in the room. No-one moved and all eyes were on us as we made our way to the bar, my father smiling from ear to ear. The bar man took our order of "a pint of your best ale please Landlord and a glass of lemonade" and we stood there surrounded by enquiring eyes and bewildered faces.

My father of course was oblivious and proceeded to try and engage the barman in conversation. I concentrated on my lemonade, keeping my eyes cast down and wishing the floor would open up and swallow me. We remained for what was for me an excruciating half hour in which I made every effort not to make eye contact with anyone before my father thankfully decided that he had done enough socialising for one night and we made our farewells and left.

The reason for our reception remains unclear, but the entry of a blind man dressed in smart suit, shirt and tie and accompanied by a young girl into such a working men's domain must, in retrospect, have been unusual to say the least! It would perhaps have been interesting to hear the conversations once we had left.

Shauna had died by this time, and although she was quite elderly it was very sad for us all. She had been a loyal and faithful companion to my father. We were all shocked but maybe not too surprised to learn from the vet that while she had been working in the latter months of her life she had been virtually blind herself.

A new training centre had opened in Bolton in Lancashire, and as this was closer to home for my father he went there to retrain with a black Labrador called Dusky. She was a bit of a character, with a totally different temperament from Shauna. She was a much smaller and lighter dog, very lively and bouncy. My father's health was not too good whilst he was at the Bolton Centre, and the demands of the training, coupled with coping with a young and lively Labrador, put a lot of strain on him. He telephoned home one evening virtually in tears. He said he had been sitting on the floor of his room at the Centre whilst Dusky was bounding about wanting to play.

In the end it was too much for him and the Centre allowed the two of them to come home before the training was complete. Following a few weeks of recuperation the trainer, Mr Cernavich, came to Bishop Auckland to complete the training. He spent three days out on the streets of the town observing how my father and Dusky worked together. On one of the days my father was instructed to walk along Cockton Hill Road from the traffic lights at Cabin Gate towards the town centre. There are a number of side streets to cross in this stretch which required my father to stop at the kerb, instruct Dusky to sit and then give her the command "forward" to cross the road. Dusky would only do so if it was safe.

Mr Cernavich however was in his car, and as the two of them progressed down the road he would suddenly turn into the side street they were attempting to cross, or pull up suddenly in front of them, or park in such a way as to obscure the view etc, all with the purpose of testing Dusky's skills. However, half way down the road a police car pulled him up and was on the point of arresting the trainer. A passer-by had seen what was happening and had phoned them to report that a man in a car was trying to kill a blind man and his dog!

My father's new position meant that he had to travel to Oxford at least once every month for meetings at Oxfam House. My mother would drive to Darlington Station, where he and Dusky were well known by all the porters. The journeys to and from Kings Cross Station normally passed off without incident. On one occasion however, whilst alighting from the train at Kings Cross, Dusky somehow managed to fall down the gap between the carriage and the platform, which naturally caused a great deal of commotion and concern.

This was in the days before there was an electronic voice to announce "Please mind the gap" and whenever I travel today and hear the warning announcement I am reminded of Dusky. She was retrieved unharmed and continued with her work unfazed, whereas my father was quite shaken by the incident.

Like most Labradors, Dusky was always on the lookout for food. When my father was staying in Oxford she was well known for her ability to beg food from the other diners in the hotel restaurant where they were staying and would often go missing, only to be found raking about amongst the hotel's bins. When he was away my father would take her out to a local park or area of grass each night to allow her to have a bit of time to run around. He had a special whistle which he would blow for her to come back to him. Once when he was in Oxford he rang home in a state of high anxiety because Dusky hadn't come back and he didn't know where she was. All the hotel staff were out searching for her and the local police had been alerted. After a couple of hours my father rang again to say that a lady had found Dusky asleep in the back of her car when she had arrived at her home about ten miles from Oxford.

There were occasions other than the one in the working men's club when some of my father's words or actions could cause mild discomfort. In the September after we moved to South Church I celebrated my seventeenth birthday and I decided that such an occasion warranted a party. My father was not keen on the idea, but he eventually agreed to my having a few friends for tea. Since I had been very small, my father had always greeted my friends by gently feeling the contours of their face and hair in order to "see" what they looked like. Until then this had never caused me any concern. However, the expressions on the faces of my teenage girl friends revealed that they were somewhat taken aback at such a welcome.

My friend Susan had a Dansette record player,

one of the few things in life I have ever coveted. She brought it along to the tea party and we set it up in the large lounge, where we intended to dance to some of the current hits. On hearing the music however, my father entered the room to inform us that such dancing would damage the new carpet and therefore we should just sit and listen to the music!

On another occasion I was accompanying him on one of his frequent visits into schools to talk about the work of Oxfam. He had Dusky with him and of course the presence of the dog always sparked interest. We were surrounded by a group of ten-year-olds who were bombarding him with questions about Dusky. The first thing they wanted to know of course was her name. My father decided to make a game of it and invited them to guess. After several wrong suggestions he provided them with clues, but they were still nowhere near to guessing the name, so he asked them how they would describe young black girls.

They were stumped of course, and so my father proceeded to tell them that the dog was named after the "dusky maidens". I still cringe at the memory and can only say that it was the 1970s!

My father worked successfully for Oxfam for fourteen years. His success in establishing and raising the profile of Oxfam in the North meant that he was invited to move to Canada and to take on the huge mantle of launching Oxfam there. Although he acknowledged it to be a wonderful opportunity which reflected the confidence and high esteem in which he was held, after much consideration he turned it down. He was reluctant to leave this country and his family and the support network of friends and colleagues which he had built up around himself. To begin from scratch in a vast and unknown country is a huge undertaking for anyone, but to consider embarking upon such a task without the ability to see must have been daunting in the extreme. But in hindsight I think the main reason was a much more personal one; he had a deep-seated fear of both flying and travelling on the sea. The prospect of taking such a long journey was one that held too much anxiety for him.

Instead he continued his work as Director of Area 2, embracing the gruelling round of journeys to Oxford and London as well as the length and breadth of his area, meetings, conferences, appeals and the increasing demands and stresses of what was now an international charity responding to both natural and humanitarian crises across the world. The nineteen seventies saw civil war in Cambodia, famines in Bangladesh and Ethiopia, floods, droughts and refugee migrations across the African continent.

Gradually the stresses began to take their toll and in the spring of 1974 my father suffered a heart attack which kept him from work for several months and forced him to take things a little easier for a time. However, after a time of recuperation he returned to work.

Finally the pressures became too much, and in late 1975 my father suffered a breakdown. The effects of this were quite catastrophic, both for him and for the family. The confidence and independence which had been such a major part of his life deserted him and he experienced a decline which was physical, mental and emotional. For the first and only time in his life his focus turned inward, and the fear and darkness which he had so successfully held at bay since the age of five began to engulf him.

Throughout his adult life he had battled with his weight principally perhaps because exercise and other forms of keeping fit were not easy for him to participate in but also because of his love of food and hospitality. However, during this time he lost a great deal of weight in a very short time. Food was no longer of interest to him and cajoling him to eat drew on all of my mother's resourcefulness. Although I have no recollection of the word being used openly what my father was obviously suffering was a deep and all enveloping depression. In his mind's eye he saw threats all around him and it became increasingly difficult to reassure him of both his physical and emotional safety. He lost all interest in the world around him, his beloved radio would remain unlistened to for days at a time. Much of his time was spent in bed although sleep seemed to evade him and he found no comfort or rest. The workings of the human mind are complex and when for whatever reason its processes malfunction then the results for the person concerned can be devastating. When such a thing occurs in the mind of someone without the benefit of physical sight it is almost impossible to appreciate the depth of their anguish. My father plunged into a dark and threatening world which was inhabited by forces over which he had no control and which he was convinced were conspiring against him. We would take it in turns to sit with him in an attempt to reassure him against what were to him very real dangers. From the time when as a small child he had left his family to go to school in Benwell he had been self reliant, drawing on the ability within his mind's eye to visualise and organise the world around him. Now that same mind had turned upon him stripping him of all confidence and awareness. He was alone in the darkness with his imagined tormentors. These were dark days, and the strain on the family was considerable. I was studying as a day student to be a Primary School teacher in nearby Darlington which fortunately meant I was home in the evenings and at weekends to relieve my mother of some of the responsibility for caring for my father and David was preparing for his GCE examinations at school in Barnard Castle. My father had always been closely involved with all of the family activities but now inexplicably it seemed he had lost all interest in us and what we were doing. The demons which were raging in his mind completely and mercilessly demanded all of his attention. My mother had a tremendous inner strength on which to draw and remained a calm and stabilising presence, protecting us as much as she could.

Slowly my father's health, both physical and mental seemed to improve. Gradually his attention turned outward again and he began to take an interest in the world around him once more. His appetite returned and as the weather improved he took daily short walks with my mother or Charles. As his recovery continued batches of letters and papers in need of his attention began to arrive from the office in Bishop Auckland and he gradually began to spend time in his study with his shorthand machine and typewriter. And so it was that he began to make plans to return to work. In February 1976, whilst he was still on sick leave, he received a letter from Brian Walker, who had taken over the position of Director from Leslie Kirkley. In it Brian stresses that my father need not be concerned about his future, his job, income etc. My father, he says, had performed a magnificent service for Oxfam and that in due course when he could see the way ahead clearly, Oxfam would do the right thing by him and in agreement with him.

In March 1976 Brian wrote again expressing his delight to hear of the progress my father was making healthwise. Brian invited my father, with the permission of his doctor, to meet him at Oxfam House on the 10th May to discuss a "very interesting idea" with him.

Sadly, he did not make that meeting. My father died suddenly, aged just fifty-one, on Good Friday, April 16th 1976 whilst out walking in the lane opposite Rosemount Road with my mother, Charles and Dusky. Like his father before him he died in the outdoors, the result of a massive heart attack. Charles and I had the unenviable task of having to find and break the news to David who, as it was a Bank Holiday, was fishing on the River

Wear; he was only days past his fifteenth birthday. We were all catapulted into a state of utter shock and disbelief although I now suspect that my mother had harboured in her heart a secret realisation that my father's recovery was not as full as we all wanted to believe. Cards and messages of sympathy flooded into our home from every part of the North East and beyond. They spoke of my father's exceptional achievements and of the many ways his life had touched and inspired the lives of so many others and they brought some comfort to my mother. On the day of his funeral his mother Cordelia took my mother, my brother David and myself aside and thanked us all, saying she had never thought he would marry and have a family or live the successful life he had. It has taken me until this point in my own life to truly appreciate the full meaning of her words.

My father's funeral was held at St. Andrew's Church the church being filled to capacity.

Poignantly, Dusky followed the coffin down the aisle at my brother David's side, her tail wagging slowly, and sat silently and faithfully beside it throughout the service. Deaconess Olive Nelson, who conducted the service, referred to my father's death occurring on a sunny Good Friday as a wonderful time "to pass in life through death".

Jim Agar had received news of his boss's death only that morning as he was on holiday in Scotland, but he had hastily driven down to attend. In a letter sent to all Area Directors, Regional Organisers and all Departments in Oxfam House and dated 23rd April 1976, Bruce Ronaldson, Oxfam's Secretary, describes the events of the day, which was attended by senior executives and all the North-Eastern staff. The letter conveys the heartfelt thanks of the family to everyone in Oxfam House and the regions. He also outlines proposals to use donations left in memory of my father for a project involving Oxfam's support for blind people.

My father's death was reported quite widely in the press. Perhaps the most fitting tribute was made by *Northern Echo* reporter Mike Amos, who wrote:

"It is no exaggeration to say that Ron, blind from the age of five, was one of the most remarkable people I have ever met...It is no disrespect to whoever Ron's successor may be that, with full sight, he will need to go some to be half the Oxfam man Ron was."

Afterword

In the months following my father's death my
mother quite naturally was in a state of deep
grief. Not only had she lost her husband of twenty
three years but also in some way her role in life.
She had been continually at my father's side,
being his eyes as she had so poignantly foreseen
in the newspaper interview on the eve of their
wedding. She had been his carer, his personal
assistant, his constant companion and enabler.
Quite a shy person by nature she had found

herself at times thrust into the public eye accompanying him at meetings, rallies and talks and appearing alongside him in the local and national press. She had found herself immersed in every kind of fund-raising activity, had taken an active role in the formation of the St. Helen's Community Association and in the life of its Community Centre and had become involved in the running of Oxfam shops. During the latter years of his life she had supported my father through the difficult times of his breakdown and illness. Suddenly she was alone and almost without a purpose.

Charles similarly felt bereft. He had been my father's friend, encourager and "partner in crime" since their childhood days, right from the time when my father's sight had been lost. Now divorced from his first wife and having been diagnosed with terminal Asbestosis as a result of his years of working in the insulation industry, he too was in many ways alone.

After a couple of months my mother decided to move from the house in Rosemount Road which had meant so much to my father but was now too big and full of memories into a semi detached house in Bishop Auckland. Gradually in the ensuing months their shared grief brought my mother and Charles closer together. Charles' prognosis was not good; his early working life had been in the shipyards of Tyneside insulating ships at a time when no protection was provided against the harmful asbestos dust. From there he had moved on to work as an insulation engineer on such things as the construction and maintenance of nuclear power stations and the aircraft carrier Invincible. A working life in such close contact with asbestos had wrought its harmful effect on his lungs. My mother and Charles were married on the morning of July 9th 1977, Ian and myself being married at 12.30pm in St Helen's Church. Our joint reception was in the Main Hall of the St Helen's and Tindale Community Centre. Charles and my mother moved to Adlington in Lancashire taking Dusky with them. They had a short but happy married life during which my mother nursed Charles through operations and to the end of his life three years later. My mother moved back to Bishop Auckland and despite having lost two husbands in such a short time she continued to show inner strength and the determination to carry on with life. She became Treasurer of the Henknowle Town's Women's Guild and was an active member of Woodhouse Close Church, helping to run a small Thrift Shop putting to good use all of her experience gained in Oxfam shops. She died on December 17th 2013 after a long and courageous battle with kidney failure.

As for myself I was twenty one years old when my father died and utterly bereft and for the rest of that summer I existed in a state of anger and grief. I was angry with the world, with the injustice of what had happened and with God. I returned to my teacher training course and although taking religious studies as my main subject my church attendance lapsed and my faith was sorely tested. However at the deepest point of my despair I experienced the first of a series of epiphanies which would lead me eventually to ordination. Whilst lying in bed one hot summer night I suddenly and quite unexpectedly and in a way that it is still difficult to put into words I felt a deep and totally absorbing sense of peace and wellbeing and despite the cruel change in the direction of my life I knew with utter certainty that there was a new path for me to follow. I was my father's daughter and the darkness would not overcome me.

Acknowledgements

There are those I need to thank for their help in writing this book. Firstly the late Eileen Welsh for planting the seed of an idea, my husband Ian and my family and friends for their constant encouragement. My thanks must also go to Kirsty Nelson, Support Relations Executive for Oxfam and Antonia White, Archivist Oxfam GB, The National Archives at Kew, Durham County Record Office, Tyne and Wear Archives, Delia Stout (nee Johnston), Mike Amos, Jean Anderton, Janice Clark and David Browning.